FRIENDLY SONS OF ST. PATRICK

THE NEW YORK CITY COUN

QUINNIPIAC
UNIVERSITY
HAMDEN, CONNECTICUT

Coigmb an n-datana
j n-ajnde an Fejle
Naojm Padpujz reo

Keep our colors flying on this
Feast of St. Patrick.

celebrating 250 years of the

NEW YORK CITY ST. PATRICK'S DAY PARADE

celebrating 250 years of the

NEW YORK CITY ST. PATRICK'S DAY PARADE

written by John T. Ridge & edited by Lynn Mosher Bushnell

The St. Patrick's Day Parade Committee, Inc. *The Quinnipiac University Press*

Special Thanks:

Rebecca J. Altermatt, *Tamiment Library, New York University*

Hilary Beirne, *St. Patrick's Day Parade Committee, Inc.*

Kirk Bobash and George Urquhart

Donald, Katharine, Rebecca and Stephen Bushnell

John Dunleavy, *St. Patrick's Day Parade Committee, Inc.*

Leonora Gidlund, *NYC Municipal Archive*

Sarah Korn, *Howard Design Group*

Michael Lorenzini, *NYC Municipal Archive*

Turlough McConnell, *McConnell Communications*

Doodie Meyer, *Howard Design Group*

Donna Pintek, *Quinnipiac University*

Diane Savoy, *Howard Design Group*

Mark Stanczak, *Quinnipiac University*

Jayne Young, *Quinnipiac University*

Janet Waldman, *Quinnipiac University*

Produced by: The Quinnipiac University Press in concert
with The St. Patrick's Day Parade Committee, Inc.

Cataloging in Publication Data available from
the U.S. Library of Congress, Washington, DC

ISBN 978-0-615-37392-8

Editor: Lynn Mosher Bushnell
               Quinnipiac University, Hamden CT

Designer: Dorothy E. Urquhart
               Howard Design Group, Princeton, NJ

Copyright 2011 by Quinnipiac University Press

1954 *Standing room only:*

One-year-old Johnny Medrow has the best view of the St. Patrick's
Day Parade as he stands on the hand of his father. Marching in the
brisk weather, 125,000 marchers put on quite a show for Johnny and
the 2,500,000 other spectators who lined both sides of Fifth Avenue
from 44th Street to 96th Street.

Previous left: **The 240th annual St. Patrick's Day Parade (2001) marches up Fifth Avenue past St. Patrick's Cathedral.** *Previous right:* Cathedral photo Wurtz Brothers.

Erin Go Bragh

TABLE OF CONTENTS

Facing: 1938. More than 60,000 marched in gloomy weather from 44th Street to 110th Street to the tunes of 150 bands playing Irish and American songs.

a Message from the Parade Chairman

The New York City St. Patrick's Day Parade has paid honor every year since 1762 to St. Patrick, the patron saint of Ireland and the patron saint of the Archdiocese of New York. For 250 years our parade has celebrated the very best of Irish and Irish-American heritage, culture, faith, values and contributions to society.

Throughout the parade's long and proud history, we have recognized the achievements of Irish and Irish-American men and women who served as grand marshals. The parade's grand marshals have come from a wide variety of professions, appropriately reflecting the contributions of the Irish in such fields as business, labor, education, religion, politics, military, public service and the arts.

The New York City St. Patrick's Day Parade is widely regarded as the largest and finest parade anywhere in the world, and March 17 is known throughout the world as a special day of Irish celebration and remembrance. St. Patrick's Day in New York begins with a Mass in St. Patrick's Cathedral, celebrated by the Cardinal Archbishop of New York, and the parade is then led up Fifth Avenue by the 69th Regiment of the New York Army National Guard (The Fighting 69th), followed by 200 bands and marching units, including all 32 Irish County organizations; schools and colleges; and scores of Irish societies and organizations. It is a tribute to the strength and character of the Irish in New York that this parade has taken place continuously for 250 years, even in times of great peril and suffering, including world wars, the Great Depression, Ireland's War of Independence and the Great Hunger.

Recognizing the 250th Anniversary of the New York City St. Patrick's Day Parade is a momentous occasion worthy of great joy and celebration. By publishing this book on the history of the parade, we hope to preserve these wonderful years for future generations to enjoy and remember. On behalf of the parade committee, our affiliated organizations, sponsors and supporters, we hope you enjoy this publication and all that it represents in our proud 250-year history of marching on the streets of New York.

John T. Dunleavy
John T. Dunleavy
Parade Chairman

a | b   a. Mass, St. Patrick's Cathedral, prior to the start of the parade. b. 1950. Dorothy Belaski of Ozone Park and Patricia Caserta of Brooklyn
c | d   await the first marchers while holding their Erin Go Bragh flags. c. 1975. Police marching in parade. d. New York's bravest carry a sea of flags.

a Message from the Archbishop of New York

Dear St. Patrick's Day Parade Committee and
Irish-American Community of New York:

Ever since I was a boy back in St. Louis, I've heard of the "Granddaddy" of all St. Patrick's Day Parades, the one up Fifth Avenue, New York City.

And now to have the joy of reviewing that great event from the front steps of the cathedral dedicated to " himself" is an honor indeed!

When we Irish began arriving in this community 250 years ago, we may not have had much earthly value. But, deep down, we had treasure indeed: faith, family, memories of Ireland, dreams for the future, a sense of hope, loyalty to friends, and hearts big enough both to laugh and to cry.

And we wanted to celebrate those treasures....so we marched. And we have been at it for a quarter-of-a-millennium. And we'll keep doing it!

Congratulations! Hail, Glorious St. Patrick! God bless Ireland! God bless New York! God bless you!

Faithfully,

Most Reverend Timothy M. Dolan
Archbishop of New York

a Message from the Consul General of Ireland

Each year on March 17 millions of the Irish, both native and by descent, come together with friends of all ancestries to celebrate Ireland's patron saint, Patrick.

In Ireland, north and south, this occasion has been marked for more than 1,500 years. But 2011 in New York City stands out as a special year: the 250-year anniversary of the celebration enjoyed by millions of New Yorkers down through the years.

On behalf of the people of Ireland, the Consulate General in New York salutes the St. Patrick's Day Parade and this special date in the city's history.

The 2011 anniversary is the perfect opportunity to honor the cherished relationship between the Irish and the City of New York. This anniversary publication offers a fitting tribute to that formidable history.

Niall Burgess
Consul General of Ireland, 2007-2010

1874 *St. Patrick's Day in America*
Portion of parade with float carrying a bust of Daniel O'Connell, at Union Square.

NEW YORK, with the ENTRANCE of the NORTH and EAST RIVERS.

The EARLY CELEBRATIONS

Every year on March 17, tens of thousands garb themselves in green and make their way to Fifth Avenue for the New York City St. Patrick's Day Parade, a grand celebration for the Irish and non-Irish alike. But it wasn't always so. History shows that this spectacular street parade had humble beginnings.

The celebration of St. Patrick's Day in New York City can be traced to 1762, when an Irish resident of the city by the name of John Marshall hosted a dinner "at Mount Pleasant, near the college," to mark the day. No specific mention of a parade is made, but if the festivities were at all similar to events in subsequent years, a small circle of friends would have met and then proceeded in a body to the festivities.

A more elaborate celebration was recorded in 1766. The first specific mention of a parade came in a 1902 book by John D. Crimmins titled, "St. Patrick's Day, its Celebration in New York and Other American Places."

"Monday last being the Day of St. Patrick, titular saint of Ireland, was ushered in at dawn, with fifes and drums, which produced a very agreeable harmony before the doors of many gentlemen of that nation and others."

Newspaper accounts from the Colonial period were few and lacked details, but it was probably one of the British military units stationed in the city (but raised in whole or in part from Irishmen) that provided the

musical accompaniment for the first recorded parade. While fifes and drums at dawn may not have been every citizen's cup of tea, the military unit apparently made the rounds from door to door of the leading Irish citizens without incident or complaint.

An organization composed largely of military men known as the "Friendly Brothers of St. Patrick" came into existence about this time. It was organized in individual branches known as "knots" or "marching knots." In 1769 and for several years afterward, the knot of the 16th Regiment of Foot dined at Bolton and Sigell's Tavern in New York. Presumably, it won the appellation "marching knot" from the everyday preoccupation of the military.

Above: a|b a. *1777. New York, with the entrance of the North and East Rivers.* b. *1895. Illustration for dinner menu cover of the Friendly Sons of St. Patrick, Essex County Country Club, Orange, NJ.*

Facing: a|b a. *C. 1857-1872. Currier & Ives. The Apostle of Ireland St. Patrick; born A.D. 373, died A.D. 464. Serpentes et omniata animalia ex Hibernia baculo Jesu expulit.* b. *1872. S. Merinsky lithograph, St. Patrick.*

In 1779, however, there was a clear description of a parade on March 17. Another British regiment organized in Ireland called the "Volunteers of Ireland" had arrived in New York in June of the previous year. St. Patrick's Day provided the regiment with the first opportunity to display itself as an ethnically Irish unit.

"Last Wednesday, the anniversary of Saint Patrick was celebrated by the natives of that kingdom with their accustomed hilarity. The Volunteers of Ireland, preceded by their band of music, marched into the city and formed before the House of their colonel, Francis Lord Rawdon, who put himself at their head, and after paying his compliments to his

excellency, General Wilhelm von Knyphausen, and to General Valentine Jones, accompanied them to the Bowery, where a dinner for 500 was provided. After the men were seated and had proceeded to the enjoyment of a noble banquet, the officers returned to town and dined with his lordship. The soldierly appearance of the men, their order of march, hand in hand, being all natives of Ireland, had a striking effect; and many of their countrymen joined them."

In 1795 the Federal Intelligencer reported that the 1st Battalion, 27th Regiment, presumably a unit composed of soldiers of Irish background, would parade on the 17th (St. Patrick's Day) in complete uniform. The

American Minerva reported in 1796 that the New York Hibernian Volunteers, a new military corps, celebrated the day and had a dinner at Byrne's Hotel.

It was not until the 1820s that newspapers began to cover the St. Patrick's Day Parade as a newsworthy event. Initially, individual Irish societies held their own distinct parades, always in connection with a dinner or a service at one of the Roman Catholic churches. In the 1830s and '40s, the individual societies began to combine for a single parade that increased in the number of marching societies and the number of paraders from year to year.

Facing: C. 1874. Lithograph showing scenes such as the birth of St. Patrick, his arrival in Ireland, the "evils of intemperance," the sun rising over a new society embracing the values of temperance, (dance and tea parties) and the typical processions that mark St. Patrick's Day.

Above: a|b|c|d a. 1871. Gallowglass marchers. b. St. Patrick's Cathedral, Mott St. c. Line drawing, St. Patrick. d. 1853. Review of the military by the Mayor and Corporation of New York, on St. Patrick's Day.

MARCHING AROUND *the* CITY

The early parades in the 1820s and '30s were in a sense neighborhood parades because the organizations met and paraded close to where most of the members lived. The tradition of neighborhood parades persisted for many years. Individual branches of the Ancient Order of Hibernians were especially partial to parading in their local areas before marching to a central assembly point for the big parade. These neighborhood parades continued until officially banned by the Manhattan Hibernians in 1910. Local parades did continue from time to time outside of Manhattan, especially in Brooklyn, which usually held a small parade around Borough Hall before crossing to Manhattan by ferry or later by subway. Brooklynites last marched in St. Patrick's Day local Brooklyn parades in the late 1930s. The Queens County Ancient Order of Hibernians had the most notable local parade of all time when in 1909, members marched across the Queensborough Bridge. The AOH became the first organization ever to use the bridge to rendezvous with the main parade on Fifth Avenue.

For as long as anyone can remember, the big parade has been on Fifth Avenue, but this has been the route only since 1888. With so many different societies and individual branches of the AOH, the parade route was often a point of contention as each neighborhood vied to bring the procession through its local streets. Consequently, although the parade usually passed through Broadway, the Bowery and Union Square, the actual route changed from year to year.

a|b|c
d|e|f a. *1871. Irish World newspaper ad for parade coverage.* b. *1893. Greenwich Village's Washington Square arch was a starting point for parades in the early 19th century.* c. *Review by clergy and AOH officers.* d. *C. 1900. The Bowery.* e. *1895. Parade.* f. *C. 1893. Union Square, from the southwest.*

Facing: *Early map of lower Manhattan.*

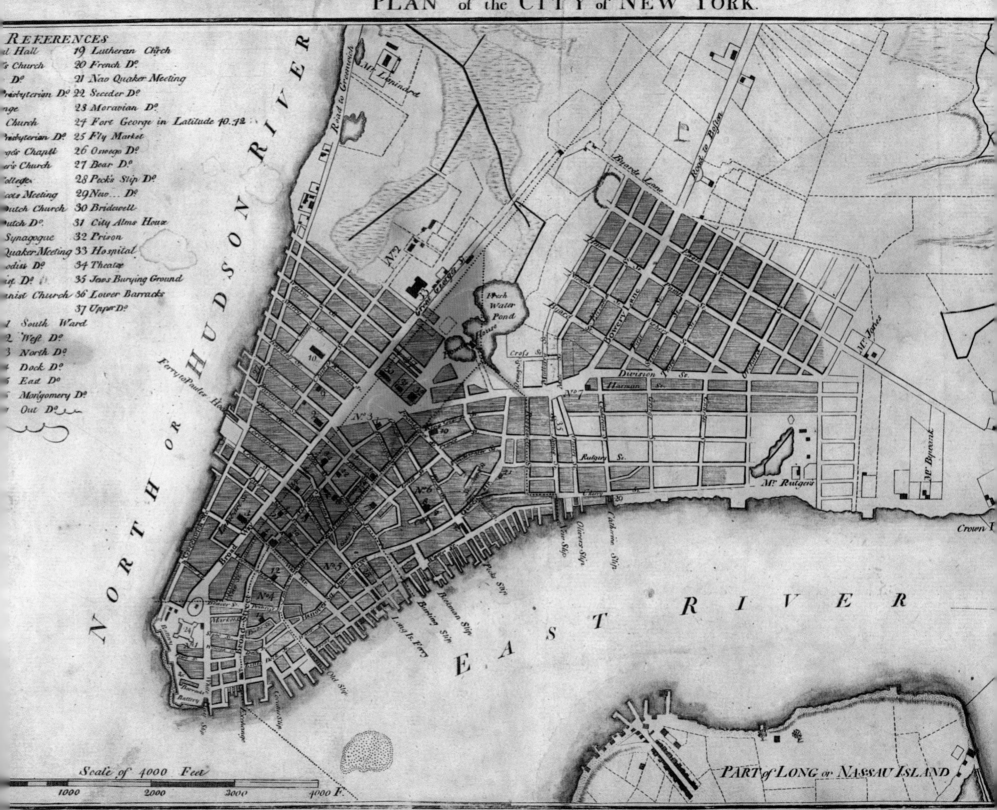

PLAN of the CITY of NEW YORK.

REFERENCES

l Hall	19 Lutheran Church
's Church	20 French D.º
D.º	21 Nao Quaker Meeting
resbyterian D.º	22 Seceder D.º
nge	23 Moravian D.º
Church	24 Fort George in Latitude 40.42
resbyterian D.º	25 Fly Market
ge's Chaptl	26 Oswego D.º
r's Church	27 Bear D.º
ollege	28 Peck's Slip D.º
ots Meeting	29 Nao... D.º
utch Church	30 Bridewell
utch D.º	31 City Alms House
Synagogue	32 Prison
Quaker Meeting	33 Hospital
odist D.º	34 Theatre
st. D.º	35 Jews Burying Ground
nist Church	36 Lower Barracks
	37 Upper D.º

1 South Ward
2 West D.º
3 North D.º
4 Dock D.º
5 East D.º
6 Montgomery D.º
7 Out D.º

NORTH or HUDSON RIVER

Road to Greenwich

Mr Lispinard

Fresh Water Pond

Fort George

Road to Boston

Bayards Lane

Bowery Lane

Mr Jones

Mr Byvanck

Division St.

Harman St.

Cross St.

Rutgers St.

Mr Rutgers

Crown

Ferry to Pauler Ho.

Scale of 4000 Feet

1000   2000   3000   4000 F.

EAST RIVER

PART of LONG or NASSAU ISLAND

Jun.ʳ Del.ᵗ

St. Pat. Parade '09   670-13

THE PROCESSION OF IRISH CITIZENS PASSING THE CITY HALL, NEW YORK, ON ST. PATRICK'S DAY.

Occasionally, the vagaries of the route could confuse even the paraders, such as in 1883:

"The route laid down by the grand marshal was up Fourth Avenue to 17th Street, and Inspector Thorne, with a large body of police, had cleared the avenue and massed the spectators at Union Square on the east side of the park. Instead of marching up the avenue to 17th Street, the crowd in the park, noticing this flank movement, made a grand rush across to Broadway. In the general scramble to secure good position, women and children were overturned, and a general scene of confusion followed. The most disastrous effects of this change in the advertised route, however, were on the procession itself. The police had made no effort to keep Broadway clear for the march, and the result was that teams, horse cars, and every variety of vehicle broke through the lines. The societies struggled up Broadway in sections, passing the mayor at the reviewing stand in 17th Street with wide gaps between them."

One of the incentives to move the parade from the lower part of the city and up Fifth Avenue was the post-parade festivities held first at Jones' Wood at Avenue A and 69th Street and in later years at Sulzer's Harlem River Park, 127th Street and Second Avenue. Funds were raised in this manner for a number of charitable causes, and the two picnic grounds were a convenient place of refreshment after a long march. What was probably the longest parade in history took place in 1899 when some of the parading units marched from 26th Street and Fifth Avenue all the way to Brommer's Union Park at 133rd Street and Willis Avenue in the Bronx. The post-parade picnics ended during World War I, and the parade finally settled down to just a march up Fifth Avenue from 43rd Street. In 1923 the parade was shortened to 110th Street and to 86th Street in the 1950s. To keep uptown traffic moving, the city further restricted the parade in 2001 by mandating a termination point at Fifth Avenue and 86th Street.

1852. _____ 1896.
Convention of
IRISH SOCIETIES.
GRAND ANNUAL
PARADE AND PICNIC.
AT
LION PARK,
108th Street and Columbus Ave..
ON
ST. PATRICK'S DAY,
TUESDAY, MARCH 17.

Previous Spread: *1909. Images from glass negatives of parade.* Facing: *1861. The Kerrymen's Patriotic and Benevolent Association passing City Hall, on St. Patrick's Day.*

Above: *1896. Ads promoting a host of Irish events related to the parade were frequent at the turn of the century.* *page 23*

elitists. An early example of the sarcastic negative portrayal by the press came in 1838 when the New York Herald published this account:

"Don't forget the holy religious services at the cathedral today. Formerly the warm-hearted sons of Erin celebrated St. Patrick's Day with beautiful broken heads, picturesque bloody noses and enchanting shillelaghs. Since the new age of religion began under the auspices of the Herald, all this is changed. They are now pious, peaceable, poetical and pretty. A capital change truly."

While the stings of the press would wound the sensibilities of the Irish, two years — 1854 and 1855 — saw physical danger from the militant anti-Irish movement called the "Know Nothings." The marching ranks were threatened, and Irish spectators along the parade route were also vulnerable because many wore distinctive sprigs of shamrock in their hats or bonnets. The New York Weekly Herald reported in 1854 how feelings ran in the city:

"There were rumors flying about in the morning that there would be some difficulty during the day,

understood that many who viewed the procession were armed, in case of any emergency. We are happy to say all such rumors as the above proved foolish and false as the whole day passed pleasantly, without attempted disturbances of any kind."

The following year the Herald reported that a large number of rowdies from Philadelphia and other places were in the city intent on a disturbance. Thankfully the large police force kept everyone in place. Although the so-called "Know Nothings" had elected their anti-Irish, anti-Catholic candidates to public office in several cities, they did not succeed in disrupting the parade.

The American Civil War in the 1860s actually strengthened the parade. Because so many Irish soldiers defended the union, a new attitude toward the Irish emerged that was much more sympathetic. In the late 1870s, however, the Ancient Order of Hibernians, which contributed by far the largest marching contingent, came under fire in the press and from many Roman Catholic bishops over the "Molly Maguires," an alleged secret society operating in the Pennsylvania coalfields that used violence to achieve its ends in labor disputes. Mine bosses accused the AOH

their public image. A gradual withdrawal of other Irish and Catholic societies from the ranks left the AOH as virtually the only parading society on St. Patrick's Day. The agricultural distress in Ireland caused by the poor harvest in 1880 and the strife over land reform brought further opposition to the AOH and its parade. An internal split in the Hibernians that lasted until 1898 caused additional weakness; on several occasions in the 1880s, the parade barely survived.

With unity restored in the Hibernians, the hierarchy of the New York Archdiocese began to formally review the parade in the 1890s. In 1901 the parade diverted down 50th Street to pass the residence of Archbishop Michael Augustine Corrigan and then returned to Fifth Avenue via Madison and 51st Street. In 1908 a formal reviewing stand was erected outside the residence of the new archbishop, John Farley, where dozens of members of the city's clergy joined him. Farley was an old friend of the parade, having personally attended almost 40 of them. In 1910 he allowed the reviewing stand to be erected directly in front of the cathedral on Fifth Avenue.

Facing: *1913. Archbishop Farley and others review the parade.*

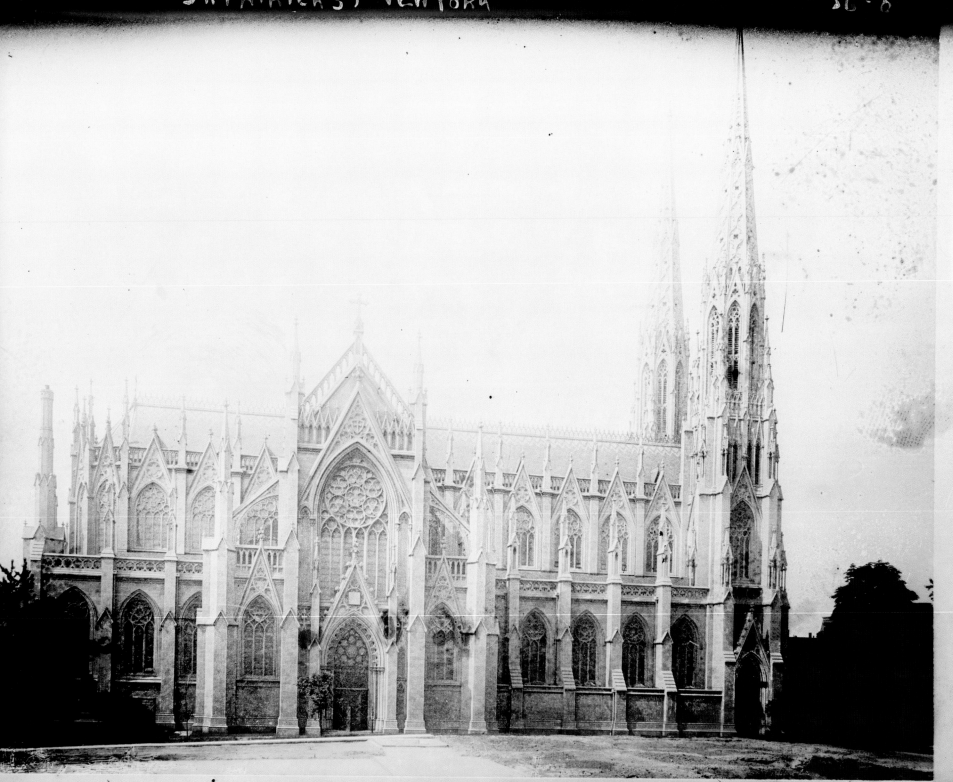

LEADING *the* BIG PARADE

The first grand marshal was selected in 1843, but it became an annual tradition in 1851. For close to 70 years afterward, nobody paid much attention to the person chosen to lead the marching contingents. Grand marshals always were selected from the leaders of the participating organizations, mainly the Ancient Order of Hibernians, but none of these individuals were widely known outside the ranks of the AOH membership. They were just "ordinary men" whose occupations included blacksmith, boot and shoe dealer, contractor, city inspector, roofer, furniture store manager and real estate broker.

By 1916, the First World War was being fought fiercely in Europe, and many Americans were agitating for American entry on the side of Britain. Irish nationalist sympathizers in New York, however, were expecting an armed rising in Ireland against British rule, while American public opinion was tilting more and more in favor of Britain and her allies. Mayor John Purroy Mitchel, although the grandson of one of Ireland's greatest patriots, was a vehement supporter of the British cause and decided to use the power of the New York government to award the parade permit to a few individuals who shared his pro-British views. This new parade committee, although facing a boycott from most of the Irish societies of the city, named city coroner Timothy Healy (a Mitchel appointee), as its grand marshal.

Although the regular parade committee won back control of the parade by 1918, the selected grand marshals from this time were increasingly recognized figures from public life, at first judges and politicians, but later clergymen, businessmen and officers of the military. The selection of prominent individuals gave the parade a bit more standing and helped prevent another political coup against it by city politicians. The parade stepped out of the parochial world of the Irish community and onto the stage of large New York big public events. Well-known individuals like Gov. Alfred E. Smith, Mayor James "Jimmy" Walker, New York State Attorney General John J. Bennett, Judge (soon to be mayor) William O'Dwyer and Brig. Gen. John J. Mangan were some of the more prominent grand marshals in the 1920s through the 1940s.

Until World War I, delegates of the Hibernian divisions chose the grand marshal in closed-door sessions, but when political factions formed upon the outbreak of civil war in Ireland in 1922, the choice of grand marshal once again reverted to the parade committee. The New York supporters of the contending sides in the Irish Civil War were deeply at odds, and the resulting strife crippled the old cooperation between the New York Irish societies. The choice of grand marshals consequently had far more to do with American than with Irish politics because grand marshals over the next few decades were most commonly New York Supreme Court judges or political office holders.

Parade issues that reflected Irish politics served as lightning rods for media attention and criticism. The selection in 1983 of Michael Flannery, a long-time leader of various New York Irish societies and prominent supporter of the Irish Republican Army in Ireland, caused a newspaper field day. A few organizations and individuals boycotted the parade, and the Cardinal disappeared from the steps of the cathedral when Flannery passed by. For most observers, little had changed. Some long-time experts on the New York Irish believed that too much was made of the significance of grand marshals. Irish Echo publisher John Grimes stated: "Usually nobody notices the grand marshals; usually their uncles give them a clap."

Previous: l. *C. 1900. Pach Bros. photograph of north view of the Cathedral.* r. *1913. Marchers at 53rd Street.*

a | b
c | d

a. *1998. Grand Marshal Albert Reynolds, Taoiseach of Ireland from 1992-1994.* b. *C. 1927. Longtime parade chairman Roderick Kennedy (l) believed to be with Grand Marshal Judge Thomas Churchill.* c. *1909. Grand Marshal Patrick J. Gilroy.* d. *1971. Grand Marshal Patrick Grimes.*

Grand Marshals

EIGHTEEN FIFTY-ONE TO TWO THOUSAND TEN

1851 Captain Patrick Kerrigan	1879 James Haggerty	1904 William H. Lynch	1931 John F. Curry	1957 Judge James J. Comerford	1985 Controller Peter King
1852 Patrick Dee	1880 Peter Halpin	1905 Edward P. Gilgar	1932 Mayor James Walker	1958 Timothy J. Driscoll	1986 Alfred O'Hagan
1853 Thomas McKiernan	1881 John Lenihan	1906 Martin J. Kane	1933 Roderick J. Kennedy	1959 William J. O'Brien	1987 John Lawe
1854 Peter R. Gaynor	1882 Patick Napoleon Oakley	1907 Frank Joyce	1934 Judge Timothy A. Leary	1960 John F. Geoghan	1988 William Burke
1855 Stephen O'Hara	1883 Thomas Maguire	1908 Peter J. Molloy	1935 John J. Walsh	1961 Bor. Pres. John (Pat) Clancy	1989 Dorothy Hayden Cudahy
1856 John Daugherty	1884 Patrick M. Mallon	1909 Patrick J. Gilroy	1936 Att. Gen. John J. Bennett	1962 James A. Farley	1990 Edward Sheehan
1857 James Keelan	1885 Edward Ennis Patrick J. Rodgers★★★	1910 James Doris	1937 Judge William T. Collins	1963 General Martin H. Meaney	1991 Mary Holt Moore
1858 Thomas Kiernan Patrick McCoy★★★	1886 Thomas O'Connell Michael Gilmartin★	1911 Peter E. Murphy	1938 Judge William O'Dwyer	1964 Rev. Sean S. Reid	1992 Cornelius "Connie" Dolan
1859 James Sandford	1887 Thomas Fitzpatrick John Lennon★★★	1912 Frank J. Hartin	1939 Msgr. Michael J. Lavelle	1965 David Sullivan	1993 No Grand Marshal★★★★
1860 Judge Michael Connolly		1913 Michael J. Connaughton	1940 Judge Christopher J. McGrath	1966 Frank D. O'Connor	1994 Congressman Thomas Manton
1861 Owen Keenan	1888 Edward Dowdall James Carroll★★★	1914 Eugene J. Flood	1941 John J. Splain	1967 Lt. Gov. Malcolm Wilson	1995 Cardinal John O'Connor
1862 Edward L. Carey	1889 John A. Hernan	1915 Michael J. Brown	1942 John J. McCarthy	1968 John V. Lynch	1996 William J. Flynn
1863 John Kane	1890 James Lamb	1916 Timothy Healy Major Joseph E. Berry★★	1943 Brig. Gen. John J. Mangan	1969 Rev. John Barry	1997 John L. Lahey
1864 Denis Meagher	1891 John Mulqueen John McGlynn★★★	1917 Patrick J. Collins	1944 Capt. Stephen J. Meany, SJ.	1970 John "Kerry" O'Donnell	1998 Albert Reynolds
1865 John Tucker		1918 Charles F. Connolly	1945 Msgr. Patrick J. O'Donnell	1971 Patrick J. Grimes	1999 Maureen O'Hara
1866 John Therry	1892 John J. Hickey	1919 Judge John Goff	1946 John S. Burke	1972 Alfred Y. Morgan	2000 Dr. Kevin Cahill
1867 Patrick Sullivan	1893 Michael L. Burke	1920 Judge Daniel F. Cohalan	1947 Brig. Gen. William P. Cavanaugh	1973 John W. Duffy	2001 Edward J. Malloy
1868 Patrick McGovern	1894 Patrick Costello	1921 Col. Alexander E. Anderson		1974 Paul O'Dwyer	2002 Cardinal Edward Egan
1869 Thomas Donnelly	1895 Daniel Meenan	1922 Judge Edward J. Gavegan	1948 Judge Owen W. Bohan	1975 Pol.Comm. Michael J. Codd	2003 James G. O'Connor
1870 James Reilly	1896 Dominick J. Connaughton	1923 Judge William P. Burr	1949 John A. Coleman, Jr.		2004 Thomas W. Gleason
1871 Michael McNierney	1897 Timothy M. Moriarty	1924 Col. Timothy J. Moynahan	1950 Pol. Comm. William O'Brien	1976 Governor Hugh Carey	2005 Denis P. Kelleher
1872 Owen Hunt	1898 Patrick Casserly	1925 Governor Alfred E. Smith		1977 Councilman Thomas Cuite	2006 Timothy J. Rooney
1873 John Gilligan	1899 Patrick H. Lennon Jeremiah Cronin★★★	1926 State Sen. Peter J. McGarry	1951 Rev. Donal O'Callaghan	1978 James "Barney" Ferguson	2007 Ambassador to the Holy See Raymond L. Flynn
1874 John Maguire		1927 Judge Thomas J. Churchill	1952 Judge Eugene McAuliffe	1979 John J. Sweeney	
1875 John O'Reilly	1900 John Ellard	1928 Acting Mayor Joseph V. McKee	1953 Pol. Comm. George P. Monaghan	1980 William J. Burke	2008 Thomas "Tommy" M. Smyth
1876 Patrick Reilly	1901 Peter Lennon			1981 Joseph P. Kennedy	
1877 Patrick Crowe	1902 Thomas Kelly	1929 John O'Hagan	1954 Mayor Robert Wagner	1982 Bro. Charles B. Quinn	2009 Michael "Mike" Gibbons
1878 Patrick Casserly	1903 Patrick M. Burke	1930 Sheriff Thomas M. Farley	1955 John R. Kane	1983 Michael Flannery	2010 Police Comm. Ray Kelly
			1956 Sean P. Keating	1984 Thomas "Teddy" Gleason	

★ Elected but died before the parade. ★★ Elected Grand Marshal but his parade was canceled. ★★★ Two parades were held in this year because of internal disagreement in the committee.

★★★★ The parade committee had insufficient time to select a grand marshal because of the legal struggle fought with the city government in the preceding weeks to secure the right to march on Fifth Avenue.

HORSES *and* RIDERS

Nothing demonstrated splendor in the old parades more than the presence of parade marshals on horseback passing in review. The grand marshal usually had a large mounted contingent accompanying him, with individual units also led by mounted marshals. The Irish as a group were very familiar with horses from agricultural work in Ireland, and many continued to use horses in their occupations.

With the coming of paved streets and the motorcar, the day of the horse was numbered. In 1914 coroner Timothy J. Healy afforded great amusement as he tried to control a spirited horse on the avenue. While doing so, the rotund Healy leaned back a little too far just as he was passing the main reviewing stand at the cathedral. The animal couldn't bear the weight and began to sag slowly down until Healy's feet touched the ground. The indignant Healy managed to right himself and the horse, but not before becoming a laughingstock in front of thousands of onlookers.

In 1928 Capt. Larry G. McLean, leading the veteran contingent of the "Rainbow Division," lost control of his horse when a puff of steam from a manhole cover spooked his mount. The horse panicked and galloped up the avenue at full speed, the officer's saber shooting upward and clattering to the pavement. The charger set course directly through the brass band up ahead, scattering the players to the right and left before McLean could regain control over the excited animal.

Grand marshals and their aides increasingly balked at the requirement to lead the parade on horseback. In 1933, 85-year-old parade chairman Roderick Kennedy was selected as grand marshal. The feisty Kennedy, who had ridden steeplechase back in County Tipperary as a young man, announced he would do the job on a horse, in keeping with tradition. Fortunately, wiser minds prevailed, and the old warrior was persuaded to ride in a fancy touring car instead.

Many people missed the horse contingents, but the succession of judges who commonly served as grand marshals was even less suited to ride than the octogenarian Kennedy. Hibernian leader John J. Walsh from Yorkville was the last grand marshal to ride up the avenue on horseback in 1935. Horses still would appear in the parade, thanks to women such as Pearl O'Connor, whose father was the founder and publisher of the Irish Advocate, a New York weekly. She organized the Coppal (Irish for horse) Club in 1942 and in following years marshaled as many as 100 riders for the parade.

Previous: 1981. Grand Marshal Joe Kennedy busses Beatrice Lawless of Aer Lingus as John Duffy, chairman of parade formation looks on.

page 32 Above: *1898. Grand Marshal Patrick Casserly and his aides on horseback.* Facing: *1916. Coroner Timothy P. Healy, one of the last grand marshals to lead the parade astride a prancing steed.*

POLITICS *and* POLITICIANS

Up to the middle of the 19th century, when the parade was small and somewhat informal, spectators often would cause huge delays by leaving the sidelines to shake the hands of parading friends and acquaintances. Even the grand marshal had to contend with this practice. Many politicians viewed the parade as a chance to make eye contact with 10,000 voters tipping their hats and hopefully remembering them on Election Day. City Hall became the site of an official review by the mayor and the other elected and appointed members of the city government and remained so until the congestion of downtown forced a change of the parade route further uptown. In 1869 Mayor A. Oakey Hall dressed

himself up in a new emerald green suit made especially for the occasion along with a green cravat and a green-leafed bouquet. In 1871 the mayor looked out from the steps of City Hall on a scene that was described by the Irish Citizen:

"Before him stretched as far as the eye could reach a vast sea of humans, which was at difficulty kept at bay by the efficient force of police, which the super-intendent had detailed for the work. The balcony and the windows of City Hall were crowded with anxious spectators who took up the cheers of the multitudes and sent them back again to be repeated

to the echo. The last sound of the mayor's salute had died upon the breeze, and the universal silence was broken only by the surging and swaying of the vast tide of spectators, when a salvo of guns announced the arrival of the long and anxiously expected procession. It was only then that the crowd that had awaited that event for nearly six hours began to manifest signs of impatience. A general rush was made to the front, and the iron barriers that guarded the sacred precincts of the esplanade must have inevitably fallen but for the almost superhuman exertions of the police. Another gun was heard, another shout arose on the gale, and the outriders of

a | b | c a. *Detail.* b. *1962. Bob Briscoe, Lord Mayor of Dublin with Abe Beame (far left) before he became*

mayor of NYC in 1974. c. *1965. Grand Marshal Dave Sullivan greets Governor Nelson A. Rockefeller.*

the gallant 69th came prancing on the scene. Cheer followed upon cheer as those brave veterans, recalling happy memories of struggle crowned with victory, marched by with the firm tread of trained soldiers. And the cheers were repeated when the Ancient Order of Hibernians came with their flag of orange and green, emblematic of the happy union of a once-divided nation. They were followed by a company of boys in green, whose trim appearance and orderly marching was rewarded with unlimited applause. The Legion of St. Patrick came in good order and handsome uniforms, followed by the St. James Temperance Society with its youthful company. Then came the different Father Matthew Temperance Societies, with their smiling faces and gorgeous banners. Rank followed rank, and still a new banner with its Father Matthew society was seen advancing in the distance as if they would never terminate, and, judging by the hearty greetings with which those good friends of Ireland were received, it was the wish of the spectators that they never should."

The year 1888 was the last year a parade passed City Hall and perhaps not coincidentally the year that Mayor Abram Hewitt refused to allow the Irish flag to be flown over City Hall or to personally appear at the parade, as had all his predecessors. A campaign, inspired by the anti-Catholic, anti-Irish, American Protective Association in 1894 and 1895 led to the Legislature passing a bill outlawing the display of the Irish flag on all public buildings. Although eventually repealed, these deliberately hostile actions served to remind the parade leaders that not everybody liked the Irish.

In 1903 Mayor Seth Low initially told the parade committee he would review their parade, then made an about-face, saying urgent public business forced him to cancel his appearance. When it was determined he had hidden in his office most of the day, Low was denounced soundly by Hibernian leaders who felt the mayor had slighted the parade deliberately. Even when a mayor was the grand marshal, as Jimmy Walker was in

a. 1977. Donal McSullivan of the Irish Tourist Board greets NY State Gov. Hugh Carey during the parade. b. Detail. c. 1954. Grand Marshal and NYC Mayor Robert Wagner. d. 1986. Mayor Ed Koch hamming for the crowd. e. 1935. Lord Mayor of Dublin Alfred Byrne with Mayor Fiorello LaGuardia. f. Detail.

page 35

1932 *Walker & Kennedy*
Mayor James Walker with Roderick Kennedy roll up Fifth
Avenue during St. Patrick's Day Parade.

1932, a mayor's actions could bring outrage. Before the 1932 parade was over, Walker surrendered his sash and hopped off the reviewing stand and into his limousine, which sped down the avenue to the astonishment of those still plodding northward. The mayor, it was announced, had to catch a 5:45 train at Pennsylvania Station to begin his vacation at Hot Springs, Va.

Mayor Fiorello LaGuardia, on the other hand, made a point of sticking it out on the reviewing stand long after the other politicians had fled. While only marginally popular in the Irish community on Election Day, he knew how to work hard to win votes, and his extra effort probably helped him a bit. William O'Dwyer, his successor, was Irish-born and known to thousands of paraders as simply "Bill." Because he had been a rank-and-file member of dozens of Irish societies and the president of almost a dozen of them, he was simply their favorite son. Mayor John V. Lindsay was very much in the mold of LaGuardia; the Irish were not his natural constituency, but it didn't stop him from trying to win them over. He was the first modern mayor to actually walk the entire line of march from the beginning to 86th Street, and this was done despite a mixed chorus of cheers and boos. The following year, parade chairman James J. Comerford wisely put a bagpipe band behind him, knowing that everybody loves a pipe band, and the mayor completed his trek a hero.

Whether it was the mayor or a minor politician, appearing on Fifth Avenue was always something of a risk. The public could be warm and welcoming one year and merciless the next. If things went well, politicians milked the crowd, sometimes causing considerable delays to the lament of parade workers:

"Sometimes I think it takes them 10 minutes to pass, with all that posturing they do," a parade official was heard to say. "If only they'd just go straight instead of moving sideways on their maneuvers."

FRIENDSHIP, UNITY AND TRUE CHRISTIAN CHARITY.

Ancient Order of Hibernians
of America.

CERTIFICATE of MEMBERSHIP.

This is to Certify that
was admitted a Member of
Division No.   at
County of   State of
on the   day of   18

PRESIDENT.   RECORDING SEC'TY.

VICE PRESIDENT.   FINANCIAL SEC'TY.

                              TREASURER.

FRIENDSHIP, UNITY AND TRUE CHRISTIAN CHARITY

A·O·H

COPYRIGHT 1894, BY THE PILOT PUBLISHING CO. BOSTON, MASS.

IRISH
BRIGADE
ASSOC.

N. Y.

The ANCIENT ORDER of HIBERNIANS

The Irish-Catholic fraternal order, the Ancient Order of Hibernians, first entered the parade in 1853. In the course of the next 20 years, it became the largest organization and supplied by far the largest number of marchers. The AOH was organized in branches called divisions that usually were centered in a particular neighborhood; the society well represented the geographic distribution of the Irish across Manhattan and around the city. By the 1880s, the parade had been abandoned by almost all the Irish societies of the city. By default no one but a member of the AOH could become a parade officer or be selected as a grand marshal thereafter. Under the AOH, the rules for the parade became more formalized—and in some respects stricter—because the organization feared that a poor appearance reflected badly on the Irish as a whole.

Parading for the AOH was a serious, if not somewhat grim, business. The most common banner that the individual divisions carried in the mid-19th century bore the proclamation "We visit the sick and bury the dead." For parade spectators it was, however, merely a practical statement of what fraternal societies attempted to do in the days before adequate insurance. The membership funds went largely to provide sick and death benefits for members and families in times of need. Newspapers, however, quipped that surely any sick member visited by 5,000 paraders certainly would be in the need of burial soon. The regalia of the individual marchers was far less somber:

"A closer observation of the line of march showed a quantity of ornamentation altogether surprising as contrasted with the grave and serious general effect. A very large majority of the procession was adorned with broad, gold-fringed, green scarves, on each side of which were displayed from two to 10 sparkling gilt emblems of stars, eagles, shamrocks, harps, etc. Rosettes, badges and medals gleamed and flaunted on almost every breast, and bouquets abounded; the officers of the various societies carried gigantic gilt pens, keys, gavels or batons, be-ribboned and be-flowered. The marshals were out with old-fashioned fore and aft chapeaux."

Facing: a|b a. *1894. Certificate of Membership, Ancient Order of Hibernians: Friendship, unity and true Christian charity.*
b. *Reproduction of sash worn by a Civil War veterans' association.*

Above: *Late 19th-century reversible badges.*

Outfitting themselves in parade dress could be a big expense for the working class members of the Ancient Order of Hibernians. In 1877 it was estimated that the parade and the cost of hall rental for its various meetings cost $75,000 a year, and many thought this to be too high a price to pay for a couple of hours publicly celebrating the feast day of St. Patrick. In times of economic distress in New York or Ireland, however, the daily press and sometimes the Irish weeklies would label the parade a wasteful expense.

The passage of time can be seen in the changing ranks of the AOH. Once every Irish neighborhood boasted its own branch of the order, and more than 100 branches could be counted in the city. At the turn of the 19th century, newspapers began to comment on the "Silver Grays," the Hibernian divisions composed of the older members of the order who, with some effort, made the long march in the parade. The "Silver Grays" contrasted with the divisions of a few decades earlier that were almost entirely composed of youthful immigrants. Reduced immigration from Ireland by the

early 1900s already was revealing a maturing parade as branches of the AOH grew older and Irish neighborhoods disappeared.

The city contingents of the AOH, which once provided 10,000 or more marchers, shrunk sharply in size and came to be replaced by the suburban branches that traveled by bus and train from as far as 50 miles away. An informed parade watcher would recognize just where the Irish remained in the city as the division banners passed in rotation. Division 29, the Yorkville division; Division 1 of Manhattan, the oldest division of the order that still meets in downtown Manhattan; Division 6 of Brooklyn, located in the Greenpoint section; Division 35, the old Flatbush division; Division 21 from Rockaway, Queens; Division 9, the old South Bronx division; Division 3 of the northern Bronx—not to be confused with Division No. 3 of northern Manhattan; and so on. The Irish neighborhoods of the city, old and new, once again were on view.

a | b | c | d   a. *St. Patrick's Day postcard.* b. *Irish World ad promoting Irish National Festival.*
c. *1877. National officers of the Ancient Order of Hibernians.* d. *Late 19th-century sash.*

Facing: *1895. Members of the AOH sport the "shawls" or sashes of their time.*

for D.T. Valentine's Manual, 1862

DEPARTURE OF THE 69TH REGT. N.Y.S.M. TUESDAY APRIL 23D 1861.

THE IRISH HEADQUARTERS AROUND ST PATRICKS CATHEDRAL, COR. PRINCE & MOTT ST.

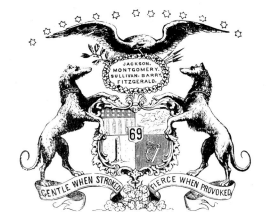

The FIGHTING 69TH

The battlefield heroism of The Fighting 69th and the deeds of thousands of other Irish-American soldiers proved the patriotism of Irish immigrants and their descendants. In 1861, just a few weeks after appearing in the parade, the 69th Regiment marched off to Civil War battlefields, suffering heavy casualties in almost four years of steady fighting. It was largely due to the regiment's performance that the Irish, and specifically as represented by the St. Patrick's Day Parade, received much more sympathetic treatment in the daily press and from the general public over the next few years. When the 69th and other military units were at war in 1863, it consequently made a big difference in the parade:

"Of course, it was not so large as we have seen it in years gone by, but we must not forget that a goodly number of the sons of St. Patrick were keeping his memory green along the banks of the Rappahannock and Blackwater, Va., by sandy beaches at Hilton Head, and way further south, at Baton Rouge, or, per chance, in the smoke and fire of the conflict at Port Hudson. One of these days most of these brave men will, we hope, be back again, and then we shall see such a festival as will warm the heart and moisten the eyes of every whole-souled Irishman."

The 69th has paraded on St. Patrick's Day every March 17 since its inception as a regiment, but first joined the big parade in 1853. During the mid-1850s when severe anti-Irish and anti-Catholic feeling threatened the parade, the 69th kept the ordinary marchers safe. It was a poor parade, indeed, without the parade's favorite regiment. Except on a few occasions when specific military orders commanded the 69th to parade independently on March 17, the regiment always provided an escort to the civic units of the regular parade. For many years in the 19th century, the regiment also lined up at the end of the parade opposite the parade marshals, serving as an honor guard for the passing units.

Many of the prominent officers of the regiment, such as Col. Alexander E. Anderson, Col. Timothy J. Moynihan and Gen. Martin H. Meaney were chosen as grand marshals of the parade over the years, testimony to the close relationship of the military with the parade. The 69th Regiment chaplain, noted in his reminiscence that the Irish organizations, and particularly the Irish County Societies, were the recruiting grounds for the regiment, an accepted practice from the 1850s until at least the 1950s.

Like the parade, the 69th had to suffer through good times and bad. In 1893 the state Legislature, in a misdirected attempt to save money, refused to supply new uniforms for the regiment, forcing a temporary reduction in size to company level. Comparisons began to be made with the Irish Volunteers, an independent military company formed for ceremonial occasions that had been equipped with new uniforms for public displays such as St. Patrick's Day. The Irish Volunteers, encouraged by growing Irish nationalist sentiment in the city, maintained the ephemeral hope that one day its members would go back to the old country and help free Ireland from foreign occupation. A large number of immigrants joined the Irish Volunteers and in the 1897 parade vastly outnumbered the 69th. Only the sudden need for real soldiers by the U.S. government the following year at the outbreak of the Spanish-American War restored funding and the consequent size and appearance of the gallant 69th. The readiness of the Irish to serve their country, as noted in 1906, certainly eased their acceptance into American society:

"To those who saw the St. Patrick's Day parades of 30 or 35 years ago, a remarkable change was apparent. The parades then had a sort of half-apologetic air, and many of the American people looked with sullen disfavor on the interruption of the business traffic by what they regarded as the celebration of a foreign festival. Now the Irish soldiers and the Irish societies march with the proud men who know that they have earned, by hard service to the American Republic in war and in peace, the right to call one day of the year their own, and who also know that the right is no longer contested. The latter fact was made manifest by the vigorous applause that greeted the marching men from the crowded windows of Fifth Avenue, as well as from the dense masses of people on the sidewalks who could not possibly all be Irish.

Thanks to individuals like Gen. "Wild Bill" Donovan and the iconic Chaplain Francis Duffy, the 69th Regiment again was catapulted into the national limelight during World War I. When the unit returned from France for the 1919 parade, it was greeted enthusiastically:

There was a storm of applause as more than 300 members of the 'Old 69th' — many of them wounded — marched along after the guard headed by Major Joseph P. Dineen, chaplain of the 69th New York Guard. More than 20 automobiles with the wounded of the famous Irish regiment followed the marching section, and their reception was a splendid start toward payment for sacrifices and trials."

The 69th Regiment became the 165th Infantry during World War II and once again, the regiment was sent to the battlefield. The regimental commander, Col. J. Gardiner Conroy, was killed in action on Makin Atoll in the Pacific and Chaplain Capt. Stephen J. Meany, S.J., was severely wounded as he tried to help wounded comrades. Meany returned to New York for St. Patrick's Day 1944, when he was chosen as grand marshal of the parade. The brave chaplain reviewed a parade that was composed of "the very young and the middle-aged with a big gap in between." Appropriately, the 69th Regiment Band played "The Minstrel Boy to the War is Gone" as its wounded chaplain, his arm dangling stiffly at his side, watched solemnly while the thin ranks of the veterans contingent passed. Led as always by two Irish wolfhound mascots, the regiment's motto rings true today: "Gentle when stroked; fierce when provoked."

The conflict in Iraq also has focused attention on the modern day 69th. No matter that the regiment has few soldiers of Irish background still in its ranks—it has not lost the devotion of the Irish-Americans who cheer from the sidelines. It is an interesting New York ethnic story that even though the regiment is now more representative of the Hispanic and black population of the city, it is still beloved as the "Irish" regiment. The modern-day soldiers seem just as proud to continue the regiment's traditions, especially on St. Patrick's Day, when the cheers for them are as thunderous as ever.

Above: *1997. The famous Irish wolfhounds of the 69th Regiment lead the parade each year.*

Facing: l. *1954. The 69th Regiment leading the United Irish Societies up Fifth Avenue.* r. *1917. Enlistment poster.*

ENLIST TO-DAY
IN
THE 69TH INFANTRY

JOIN THE FAMOUS IRISH REGIMENT
THAT FOUGHT IN ALL THE GREAT
BATTLES OF THE **CIVIL WAR**,
FROM BULL RUN TO APPOMATOX

GO TO THE FRONT
WITH YOUR FRIENDS

DON'T BE DRAFTED INTO SOME REGIMENT
WHERE YOU DON'T KNOW ANYONE

MEN WANTED FROM **18 TO 40**

APPLY AT THE ARMORY
LEXINGTON AVENUE and 25th STREET

IRELANDS HISTORICAL EMBLEMS.
ANCIENT CROSS.   ANCIENT HARP & SHAMROCKS.   STANDARD – ERIN.
ROUND TOWER.   ABBEY.   LAKES – KILLARNEY.

Antrim
Armagh
Carlow
Cavan
Clare
Cork
Derry
Donegal
Down
Dublin
Fermanagh
Galway
Kerry
Kildare
Kilkenny
Laois
Leitrim
Limerick
Longford
Louth
Mayo
Meath
Monaghan
Offaly
Roscommon
Sligo
Tipperary
Tyrone
Waterford
Westmeath
Wexford
Wicklow

The COUNTIES *Are* COMING

A high point for many parade observers was the approach each year of the first of the splendid banners of the Irish county societies. The county societies were easily spotted because their banners were far larger and more elaborate than any other organization in the parade. The counties would march in a body, one after another, except when some units are selected to march as a special honor near the head of the parade.

Although many cheering along the sidelines may have had ancestors long removed from Donegal, Kerry or Roscommon, an emotional bond to long-dormant family memories seemed to be instantaneously rekindled. Somehow the faces of the marchers looked especially familiar, almost like witnessing the approach of kith and kin. Refrains such as, "Doesn't he look like Uncle Pat?" and "She's the picture of your Aunt Kate" could be heard from many onlookers perhaps recognizing a distant member of their clan.

A few Irish county societies were around from as early as the 1850s, but they joined the parade only sporadically. By 1907 only five of Ireland's 32 counties were missing, but it was to be many years before Irish unity was achieved, even on Fifth Avenue. Not until 1959 would all 32 counties be represented together in the parade. The colorful and carefully crafted banners of the county societies often took on an almost surreal appearance as they floated by with their images of saints, political heroes or sentimental views of the old country. A big gust of wind would puff them up like sails.

Above: *Ireland's historical emblems include harps and shamrocks.*   Facing: *2009. Richard Dunne, County Kilkenny Association.*

"Whether we live in Cork or Boston, Chicago or Sydney, we are all members of a great family, which is linked together by that strongest of chains: a common past."

— John F. Kennedy

DESPITE RAIN *or* SNOW

On March 18, 1881, The New York Times reported that "St. Patrick's Day was hardly recognizable yesterday because it did not rain." Certainly, the Irish were not often blessed with good weather. Over the years the day has been more commonly a saga of rain, wind, freezing weather, slush, sometimes snow and occasionally weather fit for neither man nor beast. Many times the newspapers challenged the sanity of the marchers in setting out in such deplorable conditions. With only two exceptions, the parade has never been postponed. Indeed, for many participants it was a case of the more difficult the conditions, the better.

In 1855 three inches of snow fell in the morning, and matters were made worse by a steady rain that continued throughout the day. A year before, the AOH was attacked during a July 4 parade, and it was feared

a similar attack would take place. In this case, the bad weather was considered a good omen—the day passed quietly and peacefully.

Even when it didn't rain or snow, conditions still could be poor. Mud, seemingly omnipresent in the streets of 19th-century New York, quickly soiled resplendent uniforms and shiny boots and made marching in step to the music comedic. It was as if the honor of Ireland was at stake and marching units sprouted "'perfectly brown billowy oceans of umbrellas." Even the marshals on horseback galloped to and fro carrying umbrellas. In 1877, on one particularly horrible day, the Times wrote:

"The remark was prevalent everywhere that no one but Irishmen would do it, and it was probably correctly stated. Irishmen throughout the metropolis

cited the parade under such adverse circumstances as the strongest evidence of the indomitability of the Celtic character, and would have felt, if the display had been postponed, that Irish prestige had suffered in consequence. So the Irishmen 'walked' to maintain the ideality of the Irish national integrity, and if some graves in Calvary Cemetery do not result from the 'walk' and the drenching to which so many thousands of persons were exposed, it may be attributed to some interposition of Providence and the constitutional soundness of the Celtic physique."

Even when New York's streets finally were paved, the weather could wreak havoc with marchers. A blanket of wet, slushy snow hit paraders in 1940, making conditions so bad a postponement was considered. A long delay would have resulted because of the timing

Above: a | b | c a. *Holy Name Society, Brooklyn and Queens NYFD.* b. *Children under blanket.* c. *2000. Trying to stay warm.*   Facing: *1940. Bumbershoots in the snow.*

of Holy Week and Easter that year, so it was decided to carry on. A New York Times article from March 17, 1940, stated:

"Old, gray haired sons of Erin and little fellows who have never seen the old country stood for hours in miserable weather for the privilege of marching more than three miles up Fifth Avenue to bow reverently to the clergy on the steps of St. Patrick's Cathedral and to wave their hats at a stand full of dignitaries in front of the Central Park Arsenal. They were soaked, weary and footsore when the four hour and 15 minute parade was over, but many of them still had enough spirit in them to attend the scores of Irish parties all over the city."

1943 *General William J. Costigan*
General William J. Costigan leads WWI veterans.

LaGuardia was impressed by the determination and said, "When a country can produce 60,000 people to parade on a day like this, we're all right."

A big storm in 1956 brought ice and slush, puddles, snow piles, blustery winds and rivers of water running down the gutters. Paraders had to negotiate a small pond at 60th Street, but they were relatively lucky. When snow resumed late in the afternoon, the parade was almost over, and marchers missed most of the 11 inches of snow that covered the city before it finally ended. When almost two inches of snow fell in 1960, many of the bands from the suburbs just couldn't get to the city. Even if they did make it on such days, cold weather froze the moisture in their instruments, causing the valves to stick and rendering the instrument inoperable. Three to eight inches of snow in near blizzard conditions hit the city in 1967, and for the first time in years, there were more marchers than spectators.

As bad as it was for paraders and spectators in bad weather, it could be hardest on the marshals, parade officials and reviewing stand workers who had to remain virtually in one position for the entire parade. In 1974 the grand marshal was Paul O'Dwyer, former City Council president and brother of Mayor William O'Dwyer. A steady, cold, soaking rain came down without interruption during the entire parade, and O'Dwyer was at his post on the reviewing stand for almost all that time. When he finally got home to change his clothes, O'Dwyer discovered that his tricolor sash had become so saturated that it soaked through his clothing and dyed his chest a bright green, white and orange.

WOMEN *in the* PARADE

The parade began as a military march, and even in the 19th century, when civilian participation grew to sizeable proportions, there was always a military aspect. Paraders were given careful instruction on how to march, what to wear and how their appearance was to be uniform. Few questioned that parades were semi-military affairs and consequently, they were male-only events, both for the St. Patrick's Day Parade and every other parade almost to World War I. Men put themselves on parade not just for the sake of St. Patrick, but to be seen by the tens of thousands of women who flocked from near and far to see them in their finest. Women proudly gave their time to prepare the dress, regalia and banners of their husbands, sons and relations because the Irish were on display to their fellow New Yorkers, and the only impression allowable was the best impression. Pre-parade ceremonies frequently included women making formal presentations of flags, banners and regalia to the marching organizations. In this manner they got to share some of the limelight.

Women did make it into the line of march on a number of occasions in the 19th century, when floats were included as part of historical pageants that featured Irish maidens allegorically portraying Erin and America. In 1913 suffragettes decided to march in the parade for a few blocks, but were escorted out by the police. One of the parade marshals, however, apologized, shook hands with them and pledged to join them in the upcoming suffrage parade. In 1918 women finally joined the parade ranks when 3,000 women relatives of soldiers serving in France and a unit of the Cumann na mBan, a women's Irish nationalist society, participated.

It took far longer for women to be selected grand marshals of the parade. It was not until 1987 that two women were in the running for grand marshal and not until 1989 when Dorothy Hayden Cudahy was chosen. She was an appropriate individual to be selected for this first-time honor. As a girl she had performed in her father's Irish stage shows, which toured a circuit of theaters in the principal Irish neighborhoods of the city. When her father passed away suddenly in the 1940s, she took over his Sunday night Irish radio program, a fixture in almost every Irish home in the metropolitan area. In 1991, Mary Holt Moore, another well-known figure in Irish circles for many decades and a leader in the Irish language movement as president of the Gaelic Society, became the second female grand marshal. Maureen O'Hara, the star of dozens of major Hollywood films, was chosen as grand marshal in 1999.

VISITORS *to the* PARADE

John Francis Maguire, an Irish member of the British Parliament representing Cork, toured America in 1867. When he returned to Ireland, he published his impressions and observations of his American visit. He was probably the first Irish-elected politician to see the parade and was the right man to make an observation from the steps of City Hall:

"Quite a feature of the procession was a genuine Irish jaunting car, upon one side of which were seated a pair of pipers, each with a pair of bagpipes, and on the other side three jovial Celts, who seemed to enjoy their late-sprung popularity. The mayor retained his position for the three hours as patiently as the brownstone statue opposite, sharing with it the honors of the salutes from the marshals on horseback, and the processionists on foot."

If there were other notables coming to see the parade, they escaped notice. Outside of politicians and a few clergy, the New York parade was a local event and had so many imitators in other cities from coast to coast that its distinguishing feature was its length. Toward the close of the 19th century, some celebrity guests began to turn up on St. Patrick's Day. In 1886, Civil War Gen. Daniel E. Sickles came to discharge a duty "as he knew the Irish had to help secure American liberty, and he felt bound to help them in their own struggle." In 1906, former Chief of Staff of the U.S. Army, General Nelson A. Miles, came especially to review the military contingent. In 1901 John Daly, Mayor of Limerick, Ireland, observed the parade while on a mission to consult with other militant nationalists in America. Until after World War I, however, celebrities were in short supply at the St. Patrick's Day Parade.

Dublin's first visiting mayor, Alfie Byrne, reviewed the parade in 1935, and Hollywood film star Pat O'Brien came in 1946, but it was not until President Harry S. Truman made an appearance at the outset of his 1948 presidential campaign that the parade began to get national attention. Thanks to fast airline links between Ireland and the U.S., at least three Dublin mayors and several more from other Irish cities arrived for the parade in the 1950s. In 1956, Ireland's Taoiseach (prime minister), John A. Costello, was a guest. West Berlin's Mayor Willy Brandt was present in 1960, and the defense minister of Spain came in 1984. Office seekers, particularly from the 1960s on, flocked to the avenue to preen before the ready-made crowds, among them New York's various elected officials.

Above: a | b | c a. *C. 1855-65. General Nelson A. Miles.* b. *C. 1860-65. General Daniel E. Sickles, Federal Army officer.* c. *1960. Berlin Mayor Willy Brandt visited the parade.*

a | b
c | d

a. *Archbishop Gregorios. of Thyateira and Great Britain* b. *1980. Mayor Ed Koch and First Lady Rosalynn Carter in reviewing stand.* c. *1966. Jacqueline Kennedy Onassis among parade onlookers.* d. *1948. President Harry S. Truman was the first sitting president to review the parade. Shown with Rev. William Hennessy (l) and John J. Sheahan, parade chairman.*

1872 *Lithograph*
St. Patrick's Day in America.

An IRISH and AMERICAN INSTITUTION

By the 1930s, St. Patrick's Day was as much an American celebration as it was an Irish one. Parade chairman John J. Sheahan in 1939, in the face of the approaching war, reflected on the meaning of the parade as an American institution:

"What a difference there is in this parade — a demonstration by patriotic Americans of Irish birth or descent, who are ready to fight and die for America and the parades that are blotting the face of Europe this day! It makes me proud to be in the land of the free."

But in the Irish neighborhoods of the city, the parade was a decidedly Irish event. In the South Bronx on St. Patrick's Day 1939, a whole neighborhood of Irish seemed to be drawn to Fifth Avenue. A "sea of humanity," as the newspapers described it, rushed to the subway heading to the parade. So strong was the tide that two of the Glennon brothers, aged 5 and 7, were swept along with the crowd and slipped unnoticed under the turnstiles on an adventurous subway journey to the parade. It was a friendly throng not very different from a gathering on a fair day in Ireland, and the Glennon boys were in good company. Fortunately, police discovered the missing lads and brought them to the 51st Street station to await their parents.

St. Patrick's Day was always a lighthearted day. Early one morning in 1947, a group of reporters from the New York Daily News decided that it would be a great surprise to paint a green line down the middle of Fifth Avenue. Led by Danny Meehan, a well-known police reporter, the crew snuck into the storeroom in the News building to gather up paint and brushes; a short time later, all were packed into a newspaper delivery

truck. Without anybody noticing, they painted a four-inch stripe of green down the middle of the avenue for about three blocks. The police noticed the paint job and reported it to Mayor William O'Dwyer as a case of vandalism. The mayor initially agreed, but then saw the humor in the act, and from that point on, the city picked up the task. In the late 1950s, pranksters— one year a group of students from City College and another year, an oddball physician — secretly painted an orange line over the green. In 1963 the city discontinued the practice for financial reasons, but businessman Neil Walsh revived the tradition in 1975. In recent years, parade directors John Fitzsimons and Kevin Nelson continue the tradition through their generous financial support.

Except for several years in the late 1960s and early '70s, when the parade was marred for a time by drug and substance abusers that tried to turn it into another Mardi Gras, the sidelines along the parade route were a relatively quiet place. It was the place where old friends, families and extended families ruled the day. All the Irish seemed to come to the city on St. Patrick's Day.

Perhaps no other Irish-American embodied the public face of the St. Patrick's Day Parade more than did James J. Comerford, judge of the New York Criminal Court and parade chairman from 1965-84. In his youth in Ireland, Comerford had joined the ranks of the Irish Republican Army to help free his native land from British rule. His massive volume, "My Kilkenny I.R.A. Days, 1916–1922," recounted many adventures from those years and is a valuable source of local Irish history during that critical time. He also wrote an interesting aftermath for this book that highlighted his rise from grocery clerk in a New York chain store to the judicial bench. Comerford's career demonstrated that hard work and diligent study could bring success for immigrants with the drive to succeed.

The judge was widely known as a tough and steely administrator, and he ruled the parade committee in

the same manner. A member of the AOH for more than 50 years, a family history describes him as "gregarious and jovial in private," although friends described Comerford after his death as an iron-fisted administrator. "He had another side to him, but it very seldom came out," said John Concannon, who worked with Comerford on the parade committee. Perhaps the words of Comerford ring truer today than ever: "Without the parade, many people wouldn't think there were any Irish in New York."

Concannon, a senior financial editor at Newsweek magazine, served for two decades up to the 1980s as the parade committee's historian. "Johnny," as his friends knew him, had grown up in the midst of a family headed by immigrant parents from counties Galway and Cork. As a boy, Concannon experienced the parade from a front-row seat because both parents

were at the center of New York's Irish society activity, his father serving as president of the Galway Men's Association for several terms.

With an insider's approach, Concannon began to assemble the first real archive of the parade. Soon his articles tracing the history of the event became regular features in the Irish weeklies. It was Concannon who brought the parade national and international attention by arranging publicity through his media contacts. When anyone wanted to know anything about the parade, they consulted John Concannon.

Above: a|b|c|d a. *1990. Reenacting Civil War marchers.* b. *County organizations frequently held balls as fundraisers.* c. *2001. Irish Echo cover.* d. *Aer Lingus flight attendants adorned the parade route.*

a|b a. *1964. Teenagers paint the green line on Fifth Avenue.* b. *Terence Cardinal Cooke, Archbishop of New York with Parade Chairman James J.*
c|d *Comerford.* c. *1953. Iconic TV personality Jack McCarthy announced the parade for many years on WPIX.* d. *1989. Flatbush Irish.*

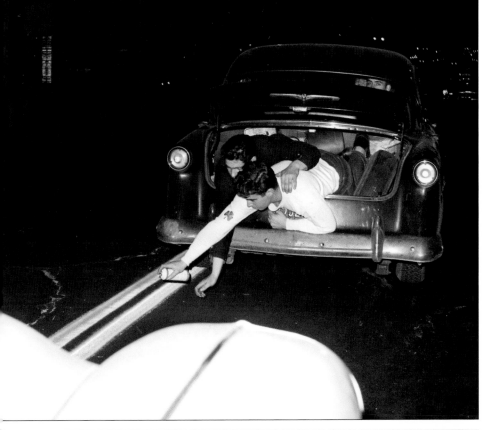

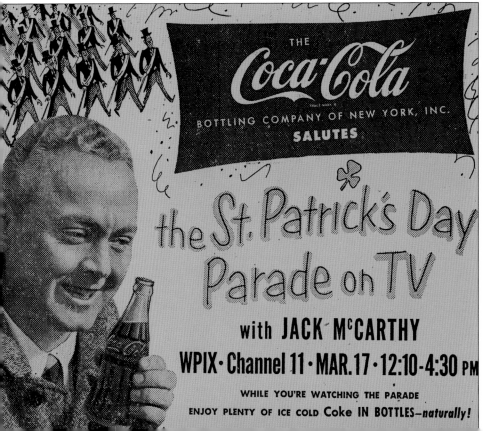

TOWARD *the* 21ST CENTURY

The city had vastly changed for the Irish by 1984. There were few Irish politicians to be found around city hall or the city council. The Irish were a shrinking minority in the city and no longer a major consideration for most candidates seeking office. The selection of a parade chairman went back to the situation before World War I when hard-working, dedicated men rose from the ranks to run the parade. It was once again the day of the genuine organizer whose year-round dedication was much more intense than the semi-political leaders from the court house. The new Irish society-based leadership of Chairman Francis P. Beirne was strictly business— the business of running a parade and smoothly coordinating such a massive undertaking. The Comerford era with its numerous political connections was replaced by a committee almost wholly concentrated on the mechanics of producing an annual parade.

Beirne led the parade through those tumultuous years until 1993. He was born in Cornamuckla, outside

Carrick-on-Shannon, County Leitrim, and landed in New York after spending time in London in 1956. The parade naturally attracted this young immigrant, and he began serving on the parade committee, working his way up to chairman and succeeding Comerford in 1985. One of his first actions was to bring aboard Margaret O'Rourke as secretary of the committee, a first for women in this previously all-male operation.

Under his chairmanship, the first female grand marshals — Dorothy Hayden Cudahy in 1989 and Mary Holt Moore in 1991 — were selected. Beirne instituted prizes for the best marching units and a chance for the winners to move up to the head of the parade for the following year. In the months leading up to St. Patrick's Day, Beirne seemed to be everywhere among the Irish societies supporting, encouraging and directing their participation in the annual event.

His friends were legion, and it is no wonder that Cardinal John O'Connor singled him out in the midst of a homily at St. Patrick's Cathedral "as a man whose courage and integrity I cannot forget, a man to whom I am deeply grateful and who deserves to stand and be acknowledged," according to an article in the Leitrim Guardian.

a | b a. *1989. First female Grand Marshal Dorothy Hayden Cudahy.* b. *1991. Second female Grand Marshal Mary Holt Moore.*

Facing: *Long time Parade Chairman Francis P. Beirne.*

John Dunleavy joined his close friend, Frank Beirne, on the parade committee in various offices until he succeeded him as chairman in 1993. Dunleavy was born in Coole, County Westmeath. After an apprenticeship in the grocery trade in Ireland, he struck off for London in 1956, where he found a job driving double-decker buses for the London Transport System. Dunleavy came to New York in 1963 and was drafted within three months. He spent two years in the Army before he returned to the city and joined the Manhattan and Bronx Surface Transit Operating Authority, retiring in 1990 as a general superintendent. Active in Irish societies from his early days in America, he took the reins in the midst of a succession of controversies that dogged the parade through the early 1990s, pitting parade organizers against the mayor and City Hall, the media, and even each other at times.

An Irish gay and lesbian organization sued the parade committee and sought to march in the privately organized parade via a carefully orchestrated series of political maneuvers and court battles. The heated battles, played out very publicly, created strange and unusual alliances, resulting in the New York Civil Liberties Union siding with parade organizers over their right to exclude groups based on religious beliefs; it also resulted in national and state Hibernian organizations locking horns in attempts to save the parade from further external interference. The lengthy dispute nearly brought the parade to an end after more than 200 years. In an eleventh-hour decision, Federal Court Judge Kevin T. Duffy ruled that the city could not mandate inclusion of any organization inasmuch as it was "patently unconstitutional."

The legal matter was finally put to rest in 1995 when the U.S. Supreme Court ruled in a similar Boston case that assured the rights of parade sponsors everywhere to exercise free speech. The decision was seen as a further vindication of the New York Parade committee's long fight.

Years after, Mayor Rudolph Giuliani summed it up by saying: "I mean, the fact is that nobody is excluded from this parade, and nobody asks if you are heterosexual, lesbian, gay or whatever you may be." he said. "The idea is that you don't carry a banner that proselytizes." (New York Times, March 18, 2001)

Above: a | b | c | d a. *2005. Mayor Rudy Giuliani.* b. *2005. Grand Marshal Denis P. Kelleher and his wife Carol.*
c. *2005. Archbishop Edward Cardinal Egan interviewed during the parade.* d. *2004. Parade Chairman John Dunleavy greets the marchers.*

Most of Dunleavy's efforts to strengthen the parade, however, went unreported in the media. Under his leadership the parade's finances were improved, the board of directors and trustees were greatly expanded, its Catholic identity has been enhanced, and the selection process for grand marshal is much more transparent. Also, viewership of the WNBC telecast is now the largest in the history of the parade. In an interview with the Irish Examiner in 1997, Dunleavy said some of his fondest memories involve the wonderful international interest in the parade that sometimes comes from unlikely places. The Santiago de Compostela Pipe Band from Spain has marched in the parade several times as has a band from Finland that was organized there by a Manhattan College alumnus. Dunleavy was amazed when, during a reception at Dag Hammarskjold Plaza, the 12-year-old son of the Japanese consul general announced that he and his father would play "Sean South from Garryowen" on the bagpipes. Their pipe band from Toyko subsequently made the journey to march in the New York St. Patrick's Day Parade.

Dunleavy was joined in his efforts during those rough-and-tumble years by James Barker, the son of Irish immigrants from County Monaghan and a former Democratic Party leader in Queens. Barker took his experience as an organizer and president of his own marketing company and used it to help the parade weather a controversial time. He often took the brunt of criticism from the media and, sometimes, from within the Irish community itself, on his shoulders, deflecting it from the parade committee. Barker passed away after a long illness in 2004 while serving as executive director of the parade.

With the end of the Comerford years came the direct election of grand marshals by vote of the delegates from the participating parade organizations. This was at first a widely popular move as it assured the selection of some grand marshals who, while not politically connected, had nevertheless rendered years of service to the Irish community. These deserving individuals had largely been ignored when a long line of business-men, politicians, judges or people of influence had been chosen as grand marshals.

Above: a|b|c|d a. *2004. NBC 4 New York annually broadcasts the parade.* b. *2003. Mass in the Cathedral.* c. *Parade Chairman John Dunleavy with Executive Secretary James Barker.* d. *L r, John Dunleavy, parade chairman, John O'Connor, parade president, John L. Lahey, parade vice-chairman.* Center of Page: *1999. The Tokyo Pipe Band.* *page 65*

The grand marshal of the 1992 parade was a familiar and well liked-figure in Irish circles, Cornelius "Connie" Doolan. Like Mary Holt Moore in the previous year, he was cheated out of the attention usually focused on the grand marshal, but nevertheless the Cork native and executive of the Guinness Import Company affirmed it was "the happiest day of my life." Before the parade he celebrated breakfast with old friends, many from his native county, and including the Mayor of Cork City and an old schoolmate, Dennis Cregan, at a mid-town hotel. (New York Times, March 18, 1992). Doolan served as a de facto grand marshal the following year as well, when political struggles to control the parade prevented the selection of a grand marshal in time for the 1993 parade.

The grand marshal of the 1995 parade was John Cardinal O'Connor, who became the first Archbishop of New York ever to lead the parade. The 75-year-old cardinal, whose grandparents had left Ireland during the time of the Great Hunger, had been an outspoken defender of the parade. His selection was widely seen as both a celebration of an extraordinary individual and an affirmation of the continuing Catholic nature of the parade.

As the new millennium began, absent from the cathedral steps for the first time in 16 years was the ailing O'Connor, and for many marchers the noticeable void gave them reason for concern. O'Connor had always been as energetic in life as he had been an enthusiastic supporter of the parade and, if he was in town, nothing could keep him from his review of the passing thousands, according to an article in the New York Daily News. The grand marshal that year was Dr. Kevin Cahill, a respected surgeon and president of the American Irish Historical Society, the venerable institution every marcher takes the time to salute while passing its splendid headquarters at Fifth Avenue near 80th Street opposite Central Park. Cahill, a former health czar in the administration of Gov. Hugh L. Carey, was then actively involved in overseeing the treatment for O'Connor, who died in May of that year at the age of 80.

Unique in the history of the parade was the selection of two grand marshals who were father and son: Thomas W. (Teddy) Gleason and his son and namesake, Thomas W. Gleason Jr. The elder Gleason was selected grand marshal in 1984 after a long and colorful career on the docks and as leader of the International Longshoreman's Association for 24 years. He was born in 1900 and raised in a neighborhood in the West Side below 14th Street. In this area, close to the river, the Irish were a majority and dominant in all the working trades along the docks.

It was rough work; job security and good wages seldom were found. After decades of struggle, longshoremen finally won a decent wage, only to see their manual labor jobs vanish with the introduction of containers moved by machines. Gleason, who was known for being both a gentle and gruff labor leader, became the friend of presidents and an international expert on the best way to manage port facilities. He had long been a supporter of Irish-American causes, such as the unification of Ireland, and had been a member of several Irish societies.

If anyone was a chip off the old block, it was Thomas Jr., who possessed the same ability to represent people as did his father, but this time before the bench. This prominent downtown Manhattan lawyer and partner in the firm Gleason and Matthews was chosen to lead the parade in 2004, just before his father passed away. His selection allowed the elder Gleason to witness the proud moment when son succeeded father in the long line of St. Patrick's Day grand marshals. The younger Gleason's legal advice was invaluable to the parade committee when it battled the flood of legal actions that threatened its survival.

Above: a|b|c|d a. *1992. Cornelius "Connie" Doolan.* b. *2004. Tommy Gleason Jr.* c. *1997. Martin Kearns, Chairman, Parade Formation.*
d. *Hilary Beirne, Chairman, Parade Formation and Corresponding Secretary.* Facing: a|b a. *1958. The Cathedral* b. *1995. Archbishop of New York John Cardinal O'Connor.*

"We entered a cabin. Stretched in one dark corner, scarcely visible from the smoke and rags that covered them, were three children huddled together, eyes sunk, voice gone, and evidently in the last state of actual starvation..."

from William Bennett, Narrative of a Recent Journey of Six Weeks in Ireland, 1847

IRELAND'S GREAT HUNGER
AN GORTA MÓR: THE QUINNIPIAC UNIVERSITY COLLECTION

MAY 21, 2010 – SEPTEMBER 3, 2010

CONSULATE GENERAL OF IRELAND

REVIVAL *and* REMEMBRANCE

Gerry Adams, president of Sinn Fein, marched in the parade for the first time in 1996 and enjoyed celebrity status as a guest of the United Irish Counties contingent. Adams, a nationalist leader in Northern Ireland, was on a visit with Irish-American groups and individuals in America. Negotiations aimed at a peace settlement in Northern Ireland had stalled and Adams was anxious to win over new support from the Irish-American community and political leaders in Washington. John Cardinal O'Connor in his homily at the cathedral focused on peace, not before humorously looking down at the congregation and remarking, "What a remarkable sight, 4,000 Irish people in relative peace." William J. Flynn,

the grand marshal, set the tone of the day by dedicating the parade to the achievement of reconciliation in Northern Ireland. (New York Times, March 17, 1996).

A popular choice from both within and outside of the ranks of the parade volunteers and organizers was the 1997 Grand Marshal, John L. Lahey. He grew up in the Bronx, where he recalled a world that was decidedly Irish. Even after he became president of Quinnipiac University in Hamden, Conn., his devotion to the parade never diminished. At the December parade committee meeting, it was announced that the 1997 parade was to be dedicated to the memory of

the Great Hunger of 1847. After Lahey's selection was announced, he said, "I hope that educating people about the Great Hunger will reduce the chance that genocide or ethnic cleansing would occur again." Lahey's remarks echoed Gov. George Pataki's proposal that the Hunger should be taught to every school child. In an article on Dec. 11, 1996, the New York Daily News reported that the British government, which had lambasted Pataki's proposal, "yesterday reiterated its 'disappointment' over the comparison between the famine and the Holocaust but stopped short of insulting the new grand marshal."

Above: a|b a. *The 1997 parade marked the 150th anniversary of Black '47, the worst year of Ireland's Great Hunger.* b. *1997. Grand Marshal John L. Lahey used his time as grand marshal to educate the public about the real causes of Ireland's tragic famine from 1845-1850.* Facing: *1996. Sinn Fein's Gerry Adams marches among the United Irish County's group.*

Coming just a few months after the catastrophe of Sept. 11, 2001, the 2002 parade was an important positive step forward for a city still suffering the trauma and loss of that tragic day. Particularly hard hit was the Irish-American community, losing hundreds of individuals from the employees of finance and insurance firms to the firemen who rushed into the buildings to try to rescue them. Many of those who died were longtime marchers in the parade and it seemed each Irish society mourned the loss of at least one or two of its members. The parade was dedicated to the memory of all the victims and the grand marshal of the parade, Edward Cardinal Egan, who planned to mark the occasion:

"In recognition of all that has happened, Cardinal Edward M. Egan, the head of the Roman Catholic Archdiocese of New York and the grand marshal of this year's parade — on March 16 — is to stop the march up Fifth Avenue at 12:30, some 90 minutes after it has begun. He is to face south toward Lower Manhattan, where the World Trade Center once stood and where 2,800 people lost their lives. More than 300,000 marchers and 2 million spectators are to turn south as well. Then Cardinal Egan is to lead the city in a moment of silence." (New York Times, March 8, 2002).

The fresh memories of 9/11 produced the most favorable media accounts of the St. Patrick's Day Parade in many years. Sad to say it took that horrible event for the press to appreciate the parade for its positive and uplifting effect on the morale of the city. For the many pipe bands it was a welcome break from the hundreds of funerals at which they had played for the firefighters and police who died in the attacks.

Leading the parade in 2007 was Raymond L. Flynn, former Democratic mayor of Boston (1984-93) and former American ambassador to the Vatican. Flynn, while better known in his home state, was a frequent visitor to New York and speaker before New York societies. He represented a force not often mentioned in the press, the "blue-collar, working-class Catholic." He was recognized as a symbol for Catholic action in public life and a figure who championed social issues keyed to his faith and background.

The grand marshal for the 2008 parade was Tommy M. Smyth, a native of Co. Louth, who was a famous figure worldwide as a sportscaster for ESPN's soccer games. Smyth was not a remote figure from the television screen that had come down for one day of glory on Fifth Avenue. He was a well-known and popular member of the Irish community and a familiar figure at meetings of the St. Patrick's Day Parade Committee.

In 2009 Mike Gibbons, president of the Ireland-U.S. Council and a former Estee Lauder executive, was selected as grand marshal. It was reported that the returned 69th Regiment from Iraq provided the largest contingent in its history, some 1,100 soldiers. With nothing but bad news in the economic outlook, the parade was viewed as a relief from the grim news that seemed to be breaking day after day.

Police Commissioner Ray Kelly led the parade in 2010. Kelly was joined at his announcement ceremony by friend and superstar Jennifer Lopez and her husband, singer Marc Anthony.

The crowds and the parade itself are larger than ever. More than 200 marching units now travel the parade route from 44th Street up Fifth Avenue, concluding at 86th Street. Televised for nearly 50 years on WPIX television, in 1997 WNBC New York began broadcasting it, capturing many of the units in the 5½-hour parade.

Today, 250 years later, the parade is still firmly entrenched in its roots as a parade of celebration for the Irish, the fife and drums of the military, and the pride and heritage of a nation.

Facing: 2002. Firefighter Eddie Zeilman honors his comrades in Ladder Co. 4 who were killed in the 9/11 tragedy. The entire parade turned toward Ground Zero and observed a moment of silence.

This is Irish America

"I sometimes think that the only event that hits every New Yorker on the head is the annual St. Patrick's Day parade, which is fairly penetrating – the Irish are a hard race to tune out. There are 500,000 of them in residence, and they have the police force right in the family."

E.B. White. Here is New York. 1948

1942 *Marchers*

Marchers during WWII

Above: *1961. Police Commissioner Michael J. Murphy leads his men.*   **Facing:** *1913. Police keeping the crowd at bay.*

POLICE KEEPING CROWD BACK, ST-PATRICK'S DAY, N.Y. 3/17/13.

1962. *Maureen O'Hara snaps photos at 64th Street.*

1945. Billy Goodman cuddles next to Eileen Virginia Dolan on the sidelines.

1965. Marchers from Cardinal Dougherty High School, Philadelphia, P.A.

Baby has a bird's-eye view of the parade.

1962. Police Holy Name and Emerald Marching Society. **page 81**

Above: *2009. Flag of Ireland along the parade route.*   Facing: *2006. Jillian Clements and her doll along parade route.*   *page 83*

Above: *2010. Monsignor Robert T. Ritchie, rector of St. Patrick's Cathedral, with a painting of St. Patrick at the Cathedral.*

Facing: *2009. Mass is held at St. Patrick's Cathedral prior to the start of the parade.*

2009. Shoulder to shoulder.

2010. Soldier from the Irish 58th Reserve Infantry Battalion watches U.S. Army soldiers pass.

2009. Ray Patterson awaits the march.

Facing: *2010. A sea of American flags.*   Above: *2007. New York City firefighters.*   *page 95*

2004. Fire Chief Michael Bradley of the 4th Battalion sports shamrocks.

Above: *2009. Onlookers lined deep to observe the parade.* Facing: *2010. Police officer Steven McDonald,*

gunned down in 1986 while questioning three young men about a bicycle theft, is an icon in each parade.

Facing: *2010. Marching units in the parade.*   Above: *2007. Brian Ahern, of the Rockland County Pipes and Flags, plays as he marches.*   *page 99*

2010. Onlookers.

1999. Reflections.

Young lass keeps warm with style and tradition. **page 103**

2010. Trumpeter.

2009. *Tall and proud while passing the Cathedral.* **page 105**

Above: *2005. Innis Fada Pipe Band.*   Facing: *Marching units of the parade.*

The New York City Council

EMERALD GUILD SOCIETY

POWER MEMORIAL ACADEMY ALUMNI

IONA COLLEGE

QUINNIPIAC UNIVERSITY
HAMDEN, CONNECTICUT

FORDHAM UNIVERSITY
THE JESUIT UNIVERSITY OF NEW YORK

NEW YORK CELTIC MEDICAL SOCIETY
Est 1891

AMERICAN - IRISH LEGISLATORS SOCIETY
NEW YORK STATE

15TH REGT

Facing: *2010. Pipe and Drums, Police Emerald Society of Westchester.* Above: *2010. Detail.* *page 109*

page 110   *Two Sisters await their turn to march in the parade.*

2006. *Parade onlookers honored the Fighting 69th Infantry, the National Guard unit that lost 19 members in Iraq that year.*

Above: *2010. Fife and drum corps.*   Facing: *2010. Flags unfurled.*

2009. Horses still grace the parade route.

Little ones walk a long way this day. **page 119**

Above: 2009. Irish step dancers.   Facing: 2010. Intricate details adorn step dancer dresses.   *page 121*

Above: *2010. Parade officials, waiting for the parade to start, look forward to the next 250 years.*

Facing: *2006. The men and women whose diligence and hard work make the parade a reality each year.* *page 125*

1955 *St. Patrick's Day Parade*

St. Patrick's Day Parade seen through shamrock-tinted lenses.

Sponsorships

Ancient Order of Hibernians
Francis P. Beirne
Division 9, New York County

Congratulations to the officers and members of the New York City St. Patrick's Day Parade Committee on the occasion of the 250th Consecutive Parade in New York City.

We especially want everyone to remember and appreciate Francis P. Beirne, our immediate past chairman of the New York City St. Patrick's Day Parade Committee, and deceased member of the AOH Division #9, New York County.

During his time in office, Mr. Beirne defended the parade's traditions. He passed on to his heavenly reward prematurely, but we are most proud to have our AOH Division named in honor of him.

The officers and members of AOH F.P. Beirne Division 9, New York County

Martin Beirne – **President**
Hilary Beirne – **Vice-President**
Frank McGreal – **Recording Secretary**
Peter Coyle – **Treasurer**

Ancient Order of Hibernians and
Ladies Ancient Order of Hibernians,
Queens County

On March 17, 1909, the Queens County AOH, headed by Peter J. McGarry, marched across the still unopened Queensboro Bridge with 1000 members and nine divisions of the AOH. It was a fitting tribute to the city's Irish who contributed so much to the building of the bridge, and to playing such a large part in the development of the Queens Borough of New York City.

The men and women of the Queens County AOH and LAOH continue to play a major part in the New York City Irish American community. The Queens County AOH President is Edward Rice, and the LAOH President is Bridget Kearney.

The AOH has seven divisions. The most recently organized division, started in 2009 by its president, Francis McLoughlin, is Division 7. Division 9 celebrated its centenary in 2010, and its president is A. Warren Scullin. Division 13 of Bayside is headed by Patrick Butler. The Division 14 president is Edmund Seewald. Division 15 of Whitestone has as its president, Michael Kearney. The Myles J. McParland Division 21, from the Rockaways, has Mark Edwards as its president. Timothy Quinn is the president of the Harry S. Murphy Division 22 of Bellerose.

The LAOH has three divisions. In 1942, Division 15 received its charter. The current president is Bridget Kearney. Formed in 1980, Division 13 of Bayside has Viola Manning as its president.

Cavan Protective and Benevolent Association of New York

We are the sons and daughters of Breffni.

Our home is New York City, but we share a love for the place we and our ancestors left behind.

We came because our lives were in danger during the darkest hours of the Famine and The Troubles. We came for freedom and economic advantage.

We hold this small country shire of majestic mountains and pastoral lakes close to our hearts.

The Cavan P&B Association, the oldest continuously operating of the County organizations, was born in 1848 out of a need to care for the arriving Famine victims. Many came to find discrimination and disenfranchisement. We were fortunate to be able to take care of our own.

The association members have seen the birth of the Irish Nation, and fought in the World Wars and in Korea, Vietnam and the Middle East.

Men and women of Cavan descent have achieved success in politics, law enforcement, the Church, law, medicine, business, education and the creative arts.

We accept our continuing duty as an Association to care for those victims of illness and misfortune. We stand by our fallen members in comforting their loved ones.

We welcome with open arms the newcomers from our ancestral home as they leave beautiful Cavan for their new homes in America.

We humbly take part in this time-honored expression of the meaning of being Irish in America and in our city — the 250th Anniversary of the St. Patrick's Day Parade.

We know all sons and daughters of Cavan join us as we faithfully march up Fifth Avenue with pride, dignity, and in memory of the noble place we once called home.

County Cork Benevolent, Patriotic and Protective Association

Photo Caption: President Mary Power, officers & members of the County Cork B. P. & P. Association 2010.

In 1884 the County Corkmen's Benevolent, Patriotic and Protective Association was founded to promote the prosperity, protection and welfare of its membership and to foster Irish and American culture.

In the mid-1960s, the association established its first home in Woodside, Queens. In 1983 the Cork Ladies Auxiliary was disbanded and women were accepted as full members of the association. The Corkmen's Association evolved into the present County Cork Benevolent, Patriotic & Protective Association. In 1989 the first woman president was elected. In its centennial year of 1984 the association moved to its present home in Long Island City, Queens.

The Irish Immigration Reform Movement was born at a meeting of the association in 1987 and grew into one of the largest Irish lobbying organizations in the U.S. As a result, the Immigration Act of 1990 was enacted into law, creating 48,000 visas for Irish Nationals.

The association sponsors annual high school and college scholarships and leads in fundraising for charitable causes and for Irish and Irish-American cultural initiatives.

The vibrant County Cork B. P. & P. Association with its dedicated membership will continue to thrive and remain at the forefront of the Irish-American community.

County Monaghan Society, Inc.

Present Officers
Fr. Owen Lafferty, Chaplain - AnnMarie McQuaid, President
Peter McGeough, Vice President – Kathy Duffy, Secretary – Sean Cunningham, Treasurer
Jim McQuaid, Public Relations Officer – Sean Treanor, Sgt-at-Arms
Trustees: Pat Burns, John Duffy, Desi McGeough, Cyril J. Hughes

The Monaghan Men's Social and Benevolent Association, with an independent Women's Division, was founded in 1891. Both groups, supporting each other's programs, finally united in the late 1940s. We were re-energized with the continuous arrival of immigrants, and by the 1930s, the society would see the largest influx of new members.

An 80-piece Fife and Drum Band that participated in the earliest St. Patrick's Day parades was organized in 1904 by James Boylan (1865–1935), who also founded the Monaghan Gaelic Football Team. By 1938, strains from the Monaghan War Pipe Band would become the official music as the fife faded away. Our member, Charles Connolly (1872–1957) was the St. Patrick's Day Grand Marshal in 1918 and began The Irish Echo in 1928. His newspaper still remains the voice of the Irish-American community.

We were honored in 2008 by the Monaghan County Museum in Ireland with the photographic exhibit, "I Heard They Went to New York." It recreated how former members passed our culture and history to a new generation in their new land. Since the official incorporation of the Monaghan Society was in 1912, we will celebrate our centennial in 2012 while always remaining proud of our Irish heritage.

County Sligo Social and Benevolent Association of New York

"Sligo has the distinction of being the first of the counties to have an association formed in New York in its honor. In September, 1849, a group of 30 men, mostly all natives of Sligo, Ireland, met and formed an organization which they called the Sligo Young Men's Association. The association based itself upon the principles of Mutual Benefit and Protection, and for the purpose of maintaining a friendly intercourse with each other, and to maintain and establish their character as men. The society was an immediate success and in less than a year had increased its membership to close to 70."

Sligo In New York – The Irish from Co. Sligo: 1849-1991 by John T. Ridge.

The Sligo Association has evolved over the years and in 1996, the association amended its by-laws to include women as members. Today the Sligo Association has an active membership that participates in several annual events from our Communion Breakfast in October to a Christmas Party in December, and our St. Patrick's Day Dinner Dance celebrations in March.

The association meets every month from September to June, and new members are always welcome.

For additional information visit our website: www.sligoassociationnyc.com.

County Tipperary National & Benevolent Association of New York

Front Row (l. to r.): P. O'Meara, M. Fogarty, Fr. Kelly, M.B. Dwyer, R. O'Dwyer-Pena, K. Bramhall, T. Crowe, S. O'Dwyer, J. Carey, L. O'Reilly
Back Row (l. to r.): T. O'Meara, G. Nugent, M. Dunne Sr., M. Dunne Jr., J. O'Dwyer, J. O'Meara, R. Slattery, P. Costigan, N. Hickey, M. Kennedy, M. Ryan, D. Reynolds, L. Gleeson, D. Morrissey, T. O'Farrell.

The County Tipperary National and Benevolent Association of the State of New York is a nonsectarian and nonprofit organization. The purposes for which this association was created were to cultivate and spread a spirit of friendship and good citizenship among its members and to render, as far as practicable, assistance to members in need. The Tipperary Men's Association was formed in 1880. In 1919, The Tipperary Men's Association decided to procure a charter, which was granted in February of 1923 to the newly formed association, now known as The County Tipperary N. & B. Association of New York. Since then, men and women of Tipperary extraction gather the first Thursday evening of the month to welcome new members, address the needs of the Tipperary community and act upon them on an as-needed basis. Each year, the association gives out scholarships to worthy students, and hosts a banquet and golf outing. Seeing these officers and members at work, one could say that "Tipperary is always on their minds."

Department of Sanitation New York Emerald Society

The Department of Sanitation Irish-American Association was founded in 1938. The first president of the organization was William Nally Sr. Since that time, the name of the organization has been changed to the DSNY Emerald Society. From the organization's inception, the goal has been to foster a spirit of brotherhood and benevolence among its members: to inculcate in them a high sense of loyalty to one another and to their duties in government; and to stimulate their social, moral and intellectual advancement. The organization continues to honor its proud Irish heritage and tradition. The DSNY Emerald Society has had many accomplishments over the years, which include the naming of three department officials, Tom Connaughton, Barney Murray and Bernard "Buddy" Sullivan, as aides to the grand marshal of the Saint Patrick's Day Parade. Each year the organization holds a department Mass and ceremonial breakfast in Manhattan's Holy Cross Church before marching in the parade. One of our proudest moments was in 1993, when the DSNY Emerald Society Pipe & Drum Band was founded. Since 1996, the band has led the DSNY Emerald Society up Fifth Avenue for the Saint Patrick's Day Parade. God Bless the Irish!

Emerald Guild Society

The Emerald Guild Society, founded in 1992, is an association of Irish and Irish-American building managers brought together by our common heritage and our employment in the property management field. While there had been an informal network of Irish superintendents for many years in New York City, it was decided by the guild's founders to organize into a club for the mutual benefit of all and especially to help with opportunities and advancement in our industry. Our members range from recently arrived immigrants working in starter buildings to experienced building managers running some of New York's largest apartment complexes and most prestigious addresses. Our goals are to support our colleagues in the apartment building industry, to provide the best possible service with integrity and professionalism, and to foster a sense of community and a spirit of cooperation among our members.

Over the past several years, the Emerald Guild Society has gained even more momentum and support. Our very successful charitable activities, annual golf outing, St. Patrick's Day celebrations, Christmas functions and scholarships, together with our monthly meetings, have proven what team work, dedication and loyalty can achieve.

"Founding Fathers"
Patrick Geoghegan • Michael Leahy • Patrick Macken • William Mannion • John Milne • Kevin Minihan • Edward Morgan • Michael Prunty • Brendan **Keane (R.I.P.) • Timothy O'Connor (R.I.P.) • John Flanagan (R.I.P.)**

www.emeraldguild.org

Fordham University

Founded in 1841, Fordham University is the Jesuit University of New York. Each year, Fordham marches in New York City's St. Patrick's Day Parade, passing the reviewing stand in front of St. Patrick's Cathedral that was built by Fordham's Irish-born founder, Archbishop John Hughes.

The university has a large and distinguished body of Irish-American alumni, including Thomas Cahill (FCRH '62), the author of "How the Irish Saved Civilization;" mystery writer Mary Higgins Clark (FCLC '79); and William J. Flynn (GSAS '51), Chairman Emeritus of Mutual of America, among others. Many of Fordham's faculty and administrators have Irish roots, including Joseph M. McShane, S.J., the university's president.

The university's Institute of Irish Studies is an interdisciplinary program that educates students about Ireland's rich literary, political and cultural history, and offers study abroad programs in Ireland. There is also a student Gaelic Society, whose members march in the parade each year.

Fordham offers exceptional education in the Jesuit tradition to 14,700 students in its four undergraduate colleges and its six graduate and professional schools. It has residential campuses in the Bronx and Manhattan, a campus in Westchester, the Louis Calder Center Biological Field Station in Armonk, NY, and the London Centre at Heythrop College in the United Kingdom.

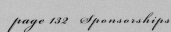

MANHATTAN
COLLEGE

Manhattan College

Celebrating continuous participation in the Saint Patrick's Day Parade, New York City, since its founding in 1853.

Manhattan College provides a contemporary, person-centered educational experience characterized by high academic standards, reflection on faith, values and ethics, and lifelong career preparation.

The college is an independent, coeducational Catholic institution of higher education in the Lasallian tradition. Manhattan College combines intellectual excellence with a strong emphasis on personal and moral growth. This winning combination attracts students from across the United States and around the world.

Established by the De La Salle Christian Brothers in 1853, Manhattan College was founded in the Lasallian tradition of excellence in teaching, respect for individual dignity, and commitment to social justice inspired by the innovator of modern pedagogy, John Baptist de La Salle. Committed to educating first-generation college students, Manhattan's mission is achieved in two ways: by offering students programs which integrate a broad liberal education with concentrations in specific disciplines in the arts and sciences or with professional preparation in business, education, and engineering; and by nurturing a caring, pluralistic campus community.

The learning experience at Manhattan College is enriched by postgraduate professional programs and by capitalizing on its location in the cultural center and global marketplace that is New York City.

Brennan O'Donnell, PhD
President

Parents and Students Irish Dancing and Music Association

Officers and past presidents of The Parents and Students Irish Dancing and Music Association together with members' children who danced in our unit in the St. Patrick's Day Parade on Fifth Avenue, March 17, 2010.

Our organization was founded in 1971 to foster Irish culture and tradition, especially through music and dance, instilling a love of same in our children and the generations to come. In 1973, under the leadership of our then-president, Larry Dooley, the organization became affiliated with the St. Patrick's Day Parade. Every year since, we have proudly marched up Fifth Avenue, winning many awards over that time. For the past 16 years, Bernadette Fee has choreographed the dancing for this event. Our organization has sponsored a dancing and music Feiseanna starting at Yonkers Raceway in 1973.

A past president, Owen McCorry, and his wife, Mary, through chairing and scheduling Feiseanna, together with hundreds of volunteers, formed the backbone of the association for years.

Past presidents John Cronogue and Peggy Clarke, and officers Mary Prendergast and Noreen McDonagh, have dedicated their time and energy for decades.

In memoriam: Thomas Farrell, president, and Marianne Zucca, president
Ar Deis De go raibh a n-anamacha.

Quinnipiac University

Quinnipiac University, through its Alumni Association, has marched proudly in the New York City St. Patrick's Day parade for more than 20 years. Marchers have numbered more than 1,000 people, particularly when Quinnipiac President John L. Lahey was named grand marshal in 1997. President Lahey used that year to commemorate the 150th anniversary of Ireland's famine, known as the Great Hunger or An Gorta Mór. Today, Quinnipiac houses the world's largest collection of art and literature devoted to the topic in the Lender Family Special Collection room donated by alumnus Murray Lender and his brother, Marvin.

Quinnipiac is a private, coeducational, non-sectarian institution located 90 minutes north of New York City and two hours from Boston. The University enrolls nearly 6,000 full-time undergraduate and 2,000 graduate students in 70 undergraduate and graduate programs of study in its Schools of Business, Communications, Education, Health Sciences, Law, and the College of Arts and Sciences. Quinnipiac plans to open a medical school in 2013 or 2014. It will focus on training primary care physicians.

In 2010, U.S. News and World Report's America's Best Colleges issue ranked Quinnipiac among the top 10 universities with master's programs in the Northern region and second in the category for up-and-coming schools with master's programs in the North. Quinnipiac also is recognized in Princeton Review's The Best 373 Colleges. For more information, please visit www.quinnipiac.edu.

The County Derry Society of New York

The Derrymen's Social and Benevolent Association was founded in 1930 by Frank Stewart, Danny Ryan, Dan McGlone, Mick McGlone, Patrick Kennedy, Charles Irvine, and James Diamond.

In 1936 they marched up Fifth Avenue with their new banner and have participated in the parade every year since then.

The name was changed in 1979 to The County Derry Society of New York when Mary McMullan was elected as the first female president.

Our present banner has the picture of St. Colmcille on front and John Mitchel on the back.

John Mitchel, born near Dungiven in 1815, was the son of a Unitarian minister. He published the first issue of The United Irishman in 1848, was convicted of treason felony the same year and sentenced to 14 years in Van Diemen's Land. In 1853 he escaped to America, where he published his famous Jail Journal and established the newspaper, The Citizen.

St. Colmcille, also known as Columba, was related to The O'Neill Dynasty and was famed for his prophecies. He established monasteries at Glencolmcille, Derry and Meath.

Our current President is Sinead Noonan, daughter of two past presidents, Eddie and Chris McLaughlin.

We congratulate John Dunleavy and the St. Patrick's Day Parade Committee and are proud to be part of this historic occasion.

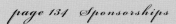

The Mayo Society of New York

Established in 1879, The Mayo Society of New York continues, as it did in the past, to devote its energies to cultural, charitable and literary purposes. One of the society's earliest examples was a reception and ball hosted at Tammany Hall on December 9, 1890. All proceeds from this function were sent to Mayo to assist victims recovering from the Famine. Our benevolence continues today in supporting education and the arts, as well as helping those in need.

The society's goals are to advance and encourage the bonds of friendship between the people of the United States and the people of Ireland with special emphasis on County Mayo.

The Mayo Society also supports and sponsors research into the life and times of the immigrants from Ireland to the United States. Fostering a fraternal relationship between our society and other Mayo organizations throughout the world is a very integral part of our work.

We encourage everyone to visit our website for history, membership and upcoming events:

www.mayosocietyofny.com.

Mary P. Coyne
President

In loving memory of the deceased members of the Mayo Society
Go mbeannaí Dia dhaoibh Go leir

United Irish Counties Association of New York, Inc.

The United Irish Counties Association of New York, Inc. (UICA) was originally named the Irish Counties Athletic Union (ICAU). The initial organizing meeting was held at Grace's Hall, East 25th Street and First Avenue, New York City, on June 21, 1904. Luke J. Finn from County Sligo was elected president and served until 1907. The No. 1 objective of the organization was to be patriotic, non-sectarian, and non-political.

By 1933 the organization saw the need to establish a bureau to help Irish immigrants find employment. This was of tremendous benefit to the newly arrived immigrants and remained in existence until 1982. In 1933 the UICA also instituted its first Feis, which is still held today on the second Sunday of June.

Today the UICA serves as the umbrella organization with representation from the 32 counties of Ireland and the Irish-American Society of Nassau, Suffolk, & Queens. The membership is limited to eight delegates and three alternates from each affiliated organization. Currently, we sponsor a middle school research essay contest and a high school scholarship program. Our website is www.uicany.org.

The UICA has proudly marched up Fifth Avenue in the St. Patrick's Day Parade since its inception and is proud to be a part of this historic publication.

Ancient Order of Hibernians, Martin J. Kearns Division 4, New York County

The Ancient Order of Hibernians, Martin J. Kearns Division 4, New York County, was organized in New York City in May 1902.

Our meetings are held on the second Wednesday of the month at the New York Irish Center, 10-30 Jackson Avenue, Long Island City, NY 11101.

Rev. Thomas Basaqube, *Chaplain*
Michael F. Prunty, *President*
Garrett Doyle, *Vice President*
Sean McGovern, *Corresponding Secretary*
Michael J. Lynch, *Financial Secretary*
Patrick Brady, *Recording Secretary*

Ancient Order of Hibernians, Myles Scully Division 1, Yonkers, New York

The division is named for Myles Scully (1880-1958) a past division president, Yonkers police lieutenant and Irish community leader. He served our division for 60 years, and we are dedicated to carrying on his legacy.

The officers and members of Division 1 wish to share our thoughts and hopes on this solemn occasion:

"For 250 years we've marched, through adverse times and weather. We've marched in this sacred parade through years of occupation, persecution, and poverty.

We've marched through years of famine, war, discrimination and hate; years of working the killing jobs that no one else would take.

We triumphed over all with a courageous and joyful spirit that is uniquely Irish.

Through it all we survived and never waivered; we held the banner high; we never let the standard drop.

And as always, we marched.

Today we remember the millions of marchers who came before us, those magnificent Irish souls whose struggles have given us all we have today. We pray for them, we honor them; and we ask God to grant us the grace to always be as strong as they were.

On this momentous day let us rededicate ourselves to the struggle. May we always band together to help each other, and bravely fight to overcome the world's adversities. May we always hold the banner high and never drop the standard. And may we teach our children and our children's children to do the same.

Whatever the future brings, let us meet it with the hope, faith and happiness of our forebears.

And always....Let us march."

May God bless this parade, all who march in it, and all those who work to maintain its spirit and message.

AOH-Myles Scully Division 1, Yonkers, New York
Organized: November, 1890
Division President: Kevin B. Ellis
Contact: P.O. Box 1020, Yonkers, NY 10703

County Longford Association of Greater New York, Inc.

The County Longford Social and Benevolent Association was founded by a group of Longford men in New York City on February 12, 1891, and the charter was sealed on December 27, 1892. The first president was Patrick Quirk; Michael Prunty is the 2010 president. A County Longford Ladies Auxiliary was founded in 1939 with Anne Corrigan as the first president, and Rose Cosgrove as the second president

in 1942. In 1975 the ladies merged with the men and renamed it the County Longford Association of Greater New York, Inc.

There are approximately 200 members today and our focus is on awarding scholarships to members' children and assisting any Longford person that has suffered a distressing event. In order to support our charitable

causes and provide social interaction for all Longford people, we organize a dinner dance on the Sunday before St. Patrick's Day and a golf outing in June.

Longford received a first place marching award in the 2008 Parade and was joined by Rose Cosgrove that year and again in 2009. Rose was 100 and 101 years of age when she marched those years.

County Roscommon Society of New York

The annual New York Saint Patrick's Day Parade is one of the most widely recognized symbols of Irish presence in America. It offers an opportunity to celebrate the Irish and all the contributions the Irish have made in America. The members of the County Roscommon Society of New York are long-time proud participants in the parade.

The County Roscommon Society of New York was founded in 1929 to provide support to immigrants from Roscommon. The struggles the immigrants faced for equality and a better way of life in America were significant. Support from those who were facing the same challenges was an important part of their success. It also provided them with an opportunity to recognize and celebrate their roots while making their way in their new homeland. In 2010, the County Roscommon Society celebrated its 81st anniversary, which was commemorated at its annual dinner dance in March.

The society maintains a close relationship with the elected officials and the people home in Roscommon.

In 2008, a large group of members attended the Roscommon International Reunion where they met with Roscommon associations from all over the world. Elizabeth Hanrahan, one of our members, was crowned International Queen of Roscommon.

For further information or to become a member, contact Mike Lyons at 201-447-2425.

Donegal Association of New York, Inc.

Comhairdeas do Cumann La Padraig Nua Eabhrach ar comoradh 250 bliain.

County Donegal's participation in the St. Patrick's Day Parade was first noted in 1860. Initially, there were several active social groups spanning a few years with various names until they came under one banner representing Donegal.

The first incorporated Donegal Association was August 25, 1896. This association is still operating and very much alive as it celebrates 115 years in 2011.

The Donegal Association Inc., has been blessed through the years with dedicated officers, directors, trustees, auditors, historians, poets and chaplains, all of whom made significant contributions to the well-being of the organization.

The association hopes to continue this tradition by ensuring it survives for the next generation and generations to come. We can do this by welcoming new members, who can bring fresh ideas, become involved with the annual ball, or the St. Patrick's Day Parade. We have launched a website — which is still in its infancy, but we hope this will be an important link, and a tool for information for all Donegal expatriates regardless of generation.

We encourage you to become a member!
Be involved, be connected, be in touch!

Website: www.donegalny.org
E-mail: donegalny@gmail.com

Rosina Gallagher, *President:* 1-718-224-3067
Sean McGovern, *Corresponding secretary:* 1-718-464-2358

Irish American Society of Nassau, Suffolk & Queens

The Irish American Society was established in 1931 to give Irish immigrants a home away from home, a place to congregate and to celebrate the milestones of their lives. Our purpose today is to embrace all Irish immigrants and Irish-Americans and promote, preserve and perpetuate the art, culture and traditions of Ireland.

We truly offer something for everyone here at the center from Mommy and Me for our new members to our Monday Social club for our seniors. We have music lessons, Irish dancing and set dance classes. We also offer cooking and knitting classes. We run an outreach program for those who may be in need.

The center holds bi-monthly dances and Ceilis and frequent DJ parties. The center runs the Inis Fada Feis every October. We embrace all age groups as we believe that in order to keep Irish traditions alive, we must encourage conversations between generations.

The Irish American Society has proudly marched in the St. Patrick's Day Parade for many years and hopefully will continue to do so for many years to come. We congratulate the St. Patrick's Day Parade for its past achievements and its continued success.

To contact the center:
516-746-9392
irishamericansocietyny@gmail.com
www.irishamericansoc.com

Manhattan and Bronx Surface Transit Operating Authority (MABSTOA)

The MABSTOA Emerald Society was established in 1962. The particular objectives for which our society was formed were:

- To develop a spirit of fellowship and brotherhood among its members.
- To encourage a fuller participation in the activities of the organizations existing within MABSTOA.
- To engender exemplary deportment on the part of its members, thereby creating respect and goodwill for the employees of MABSTOA.
- To uphold and defend the Constitution of the United States and the state of New York at all times.

- To inculcate and preserve in its members the heritage of our Celtic culture, and to increase awareness in the tremendous part Irishmen and those of Irish extraction played in the building of our great American republic.

Our society honors the accomplishments made by its past officers and members by keeping our Irish traditions alive. Our activities include our annual dinner dance, where we proudly honor transit employees as (Irishmen of the year), family fishing trips, golf outings and our annual high school scholarship awards.

Our society takes great pride in acknowledging St. Patrick's Day Parade chairmen and MABSTOA Emerald Society members, Frank Beirne and John Dunleavy. The MABSTOA Emerald Society has proudly marched up Fifth Avenue with all our brother and sister organizations from our beginning.

New York County Ancient Order of Hibernians

The Ancient Order of Hibernians (AOH) in America was founded in May of 1836 in St. James Church in lower Manhattan. The year 2011 marks the 175th Anniversary of the order in America; its history in Ireland goes back several hundred years.

From New York County, the AOH expanded across the nation and is the oldest and largest Catholic fraternal organization in America. The AOH motto is "Friend-ship, Unity, and Christian Charity." The AOH was founded as a charitable organization to help impoverished Irish immigrants. They cared for the sick, paid burial expenses, and supported widows and orphans. The AOH protected the Catholic clergy and churches during a period of violent anti-Irish discrimination in the 1800s. On a few occasions during the 1840s and 1850s the NY County Hibernians were called upon by Archbishop John Hughes to physically defend Old St. Patrick's Cathedral and prevent its destruction by the "Know Nothings."

The AOH first participated in the St. Patrick's Day Parade in 1853 and has been a large presence in the parade ever since. For many years a committee under the NY County Board of the AOH organized the New York City St. Patrick's Day Parade until a separate entity was created in the early 1990s.

William B. Burke Division Three, New York County, Ancient Order of Hibernians

William B. Burke Division Three New York County AOH has a proud history with the St. Patrick's Day parade since the division was first organized in 1936 to serve the Washington Heights, Inwood and Marble Hill sections of northern Manhattan.

Many of the division's members played prominent roles in organizing and running the parade. Judge James J. Comerford served as the parade chairman from 1965 through 1984. A number of Division Three members served as grand marshal: Judge James J. Comerford (1957), Rev. John Barry (1969), John Kerry O'Donnell (1970), John W. Duffy (1973), Police Comm. Michael J. Codd (1975), James "Barney" Ferguson (1978), John J. Sweeney (1979), William J. Burke (1980), Bro. Charles B. Quinn (1982), and Cardinal Edward Egan (2002).

Richard J. Cunningham served as vice president of the Parade Committee and James Cuggy was the division's most recent (2009) aide to the grand marshal. Peter Cassels and a number of other members continue to serve on the Parade Committee.

After 75 years, Division Three continues to enthusiastically support The St. Patrick's Day Parade Committee, and we offer our heartiest congratulations on the 250th anniversary of the parade.

Division Three meets on the second Monday of the month at Good Shepherd School, 620 Isham Street in Inwood. New members are most welcome. For information, contact jimcuggy@aol.com.

Ladies Ancient Order of Hibernians, New York County Board

The Ladies Ancient Order of Hibernians, New York County Board (75 years) consists of Marion I. Guilfoyle Division 29 (67 years) and Margaret O'Rourke Division 17 (6 years). Marching 30 years in the New York City St. Patrick's Day Parade.

The County Leitrim Society of New York

Founded in 1895, The County Leitrim Society of New York congratulates the New York St. Patrick's Day Parade on its 250th anniversary.

We encourage everyone to visit our website for history, membership and upcoming events:
http://www.leitrimsocietyofny.com.

Helen Lavin
President

In Loving memory of the deceased members of the County Leitrim Society of New York

St. Patrick's Day Parade Committee

Dedicated to Michael Coyle & Peter Cassels

Five generations of parade workers: Michael Coyle, Peter Cassels, Peter M. Cassels, Michael H. Cassels, Vincent A. Cassels, Michael P. Cassels, and Stacey M. Cassels.

United Brotherhood of Carpenters and Joiners of America, Local 608

Since 1916, Carpenter's Local Union #608 has been advocating and supporting all carpenters and their families in New York City.

President Joseph Firth

St. Patrick's Day Parade *and* Celebration Committee

Operated Under The Auspices of

The St. Patrick's Day Parade, Inc.

Officers-Directors

John T. Dunleavy	*Chairman-Director*
John L. Lahey	*Vice Chairman-Director*
Hilary Beirne	*Executive/Corres. Secretary-Director*
Catherine Mitchell Miceli	*Recording Secretary-Director*
Francis McGreal Jr.	*Controller-Director*
Rosemary Lombard	*Treasurer-Director*
Peter M. Cassels	*Sergeant-At-Arms-Director*

Directors

John J. O'Connor *President*

Timothy Ahern	*Pat Johnson*
Francis X. Comerford	*Denis P. Kelleher*
John Fitzsimons	*Brian A. Leeney*
Thomas W. Gleason	*Kevin G. Nelson*
Timothy Rooney	

Trustees

Brian Andersson	*James Lombard*
LTC John Andonie	*Eugene McCarthy*
Garrett Doyle	*James O'Connor*
Paul Hurley	*Tommy Smyth*
Lawrence King	*Dennis Swanson*

"The Fighting 69th" The 69th Regiment of New York
   1st Battalion

Cathedral High School Band, NY

Grand Marshal Ray Kelly and Aides

New York City Police Department Marching Band

New York City Mayor Michael Bloomberg

Police Department, NYC Holy Name Society

Police Department, Emerald Society Pipes & Drums

Police Department, NYC Emerald Society

F.O.P. Pipe Band

Dover Plains High School Band

Auxiliary Police Department

US Marine Corps Color Guard

US 2nd Marine Air Wing Cherry Point, N.C.

US Marine Corps Honor Guard

Family of the Grand Marshal and friends

Parade Directors and Trustees

US Navy Honor Guard - US Naval Submarine School
   Silver Dolphins, Groton, CT

Navy ROTC, Villanova University

Xaverian High School Pipe Band, Brooklyn, NY

City Council and other public officials, City of New York

New York State Courts Pipes and Drums

The Honorable David Paterson, Governor, State of New York

NY State Police Pipe Band

Marching Escort New York State Police

Superintendent of New York State Police

N.J. Field Music

Veteran Corps of Artillery Color Guard

Irish-American Legislators Society of New York State

Ad Hoc Congressional Committee for Irish Affairs

U. S. Congress and other State and Federal Officials

United States Coast Guard, Staten Island, NY

NY Air National Guard Honor Guard, Stewart Field,
   Newburgh, NY

Brewster High School Band, NY

County Laois S & B Association of New York

Onteora High School, Boiseville, NY

County Wicklow Association of New York

Equestrian Ladies & Gentlemen Aides / U.S. Parks
   Mounted Police

Xavier High School "Blue Knights" Cadet Band

Xavier High School, R.O.T.C.

Shamrock BSA Troop 236 Marching Band
   Maybrook, NY

Randolph Macon Academy Band

United Irish Counties

Joseph Duelk Jr. AOH Div Pipe Band

AOH Orange County Board & Divisions 1, 2, 3 & 4

The Kerry Pipers

County Kerrymen's P & B Association

Rose of Tralee and Mrs. Senior America

Roisin Dubh Irish Pipe Band

LAOH Suffolk County Board and Division 2

Jackson Memorial High School Band

County Dublin Society of New York

Reales Tercios de Espania

FDNY Color Guard

FDNY Banner

Emerald Society Pipe Band Color Guard

Fire Commissioner & Chief of Department

343 Honor Company

Seaford High School Marching Band

Fire Department NYC Holy Name Society (A)

Archbishop Stepinac High School Band

Fire Department NYC Holy Name Society (B)

Westchester County Firefighters Emerald Society Pipe Band

FDNY Emerald Society (A)

FDNY Emerald Society (B)

EMS Pipes and Drums (FDNY)

FDNY E.M.S. Emerald Society

Londonderry High School Band, Londonderry, NH

Quinnipiac University Alumni Association of New York

NYC Correction Department Emerald Society Pipe Band

NYC Correction Department Emerald Society

Suffolk County Police Dept. Emerald Pipe Band

Suffolk County Police Dept. Emerald Society

Connetquot High School, Long Island, NY

County Leitrim Society of New York

New York Ancients Fife & Drum Corps

Council of Gaelic Societies of New York

Manhattan College Pipe and Drum Band

Manhattan College Gaelic Society

Young Colonials Junior Ancient Fife & Drum Corps, Lake Carmel, NY

Parents and Students, Irish Dancing and Music
   Association of North America

Port Authority Police Emerald Society Irish War Pipe Band

Port Authority Police Emerald Society

AmerScot Highland Pipe Band

Marist College Gaelic Society

Pipes and Drums, Police Emerald Society of Westchester

Police Emerald Society of Westchester

Clara Band, Clara, Ireland

County Offaly Society of New York

Saffron United Pipe Band, LI

AOH Suffolk County Board and Divisions 2, 3, 7, 8 & 9

Sanitation Emerald Society Pipe Band

Sanitation Dept. City of New York Emerald Society

New York State Correction Pipe Band

New York State Correction Department Emeralds

Nassau County Police Emerald Society Pipe Band

Nassau County Police Emerald Society

Iona College Pipe & Drum Band

Iona College Gaelic Society

Iona Prep Gaelic Society

Cardinal Spellman High School Band

Cardinal Spellman High School

Mother Cabrini High School Band

Catholic League

St. Raymond School Band, East Rockaway, NY

Academy of Mount St. Ursula, Bronx, NY

Leatherneck Pipes and Drums, Paramus, NJ

Color Guard 2nd Battalion, 25th Marines

Marine Corps Composite Marching Unit consisting of:

2nd Battalion, 25th Marines, 4th Marine Division

1st Marine Corps District, Recruiting Stations NY and NJ

6th Communications Battalion

6th Motor Transport Battalion

Marine Air Group 49

US Marine Corps "8th & 1". Alpha Co.,
    Marine Barracks, Washington, D.C.

Quantico Marine Corps Band

Marine Corps League Composite Marching Unit
    consisting of detachments from NY and NJ

U.S. Navy Ceremonial Guard and Marching Band Naval
    District Washington

Lia Fail Pipe & Drums, NJ

Sean Oglaigh na h-Eireann Heritage Association

Friends of Irish Freedom

Transit Pride Pipe & Drum Band

NYC Transit Emeralds

MABSTOA Emerald Society

Suburbanettes Twirlers, MA

Park Ridge High School Band

Irish Northern Aid

Cumann na Saoirse

Richmond County Pipes, Staten Island, NY

St. Vincent's Hospital School of Nursing Alumni, NY

New York Celtic Medical Society

Local 163 IBEW Pipes and Drums

N.Y.C. Dept. of Parks

Stratford High School Band, CT

Emerald Guild Society (Irish Building Managers of NYC)

Amityville Pipe & Drum Band

Friends of Erin, Montauk, NY

Copiague High School Band

Molloy College Gaelic Society, Long Island, NY

Cardinal Hayes High School Band

Cardinal Hayes High School

Fordham University Band, Bronx, NY

Fordham University Gaelic Society

V.W.I.L. Band, VA

Notre Dame Alumni Society of New York

Gerritson Beach Bell & Drum Corp, NY

Tri-Boro Bridge and Tunnel Emerald Society

Clearfield High School Band, Clearfield, PA

Power Memorial High School Alumni, NY

Monsignor Farrell High School Band, Staten Island, NY

Rice High School Alumni, NY

All Hallows High School Alumni, NY

Erin Sports, Montréal, Canada

Ossining High School Band, NY

US Customs Emerald Society

Aquinas High School Band, Bronx, NY

St. Joseph's College Gaelic Society, Brooklyn, NY

Port Richmond High School Band, Staten Island, NY

American Irish Teachers Association

West Milford High School Band, NJ

St. Francis Prep High School, Queens, NYC

Teitelman High School Band, Cape May, NJ

Siena College Gaelic Society

Brentwood High School Green Machine Band

Saint John's University Gaelic Society

Breezy Point Catholic Pipes & Drums

58 Reserve Infantry Battalion Defense Force Ireland

Newport Rhode Island AOH Pipe & Drum

Dennis E. Collins AOH Division 1, Newport, RI

Bishop Hendrickson High School Band, Warwick, RI

Providence College Alumni Society of New York

Sioil na hEireann Pipe Band

LAOH National Board

AOH & LAOH New York State Boards

Glór na Gael Pipes and Drums Band

AOH Queens County Board and Divisions 14, 15 & 21

Our Lady of Peace, Lynbrook, NY

LAOH Queens County Board and Divisions 15

IBEW Local 25 Pipe Band

AOH Nassau County Board

American Celtic Pipes and Drum

Nassau County AOH Division 3 & 8

Irish Thunder Pipe Band

Nassau County AOH Division 11

Tara Pipes & Drums, Massapequa, LI

Nassau County AOH Division 15

American Legion Pipe Band, Wantagh, NY

Nassau County AOH Division 17

St. Ann's Pipe Band, NJ

LAOH Nassau County Board

Saffron United Pipe Band, LI

AOH Suffolk County Board and Divisions 2, 3, 7 & 9

Knights of Columbus Pipe Band

AOH Kings County Board and Division 22 & 35

Bishop Kearney High School Band, Brooklyn, NY

Kings County Board LAOH and Division 6

Staten Island Pipers Association, Pipe Band

AOH Staten Island County Board and Divisions 3 & 4

LAOH Staten Island County Board and Divisions 1, 2 & 4

Clann na Vale Pipe Band

AOH Bronx County Board and Divisions 3, 4, 5, 7 & 9

Cairo-Durham High School Marching Mustang Band

LAOH Bronx County Board and Division 9

Neptune High School Marching Band, NJ

LAOH New York County Board and Division 29

Christian Brothers Academy, Albany, NY

AOH New York County Board and Divisions 1, 2, 3, 4 & 7

Blackthorn Bagpipe Band

AOH Westchester County Board Men and Ladies &
    AOH Divisions 1 & 18

American Irish Association of Westchester

Rockland County AOH Bagpipe Band

AOH Rockland County Board

LAOH Rockland County Board and Division 3

AOH Orange County Board and Divisions 1, 2, 3 & 4

St. Joseph's By The Sea, Staten Island, NY

LAOH Orange County Board

Longwood High School Band

Mount Saint Michael Academy, Bronx, NY

The Sword of Light Pipe Band (Local 3 IBEW)

Irish American Labor Coalition

Local 608 Carpenters and Joiners Union Pipe Band, NY

New York Minor Board G.A.A.

F. D. Orange County, CA

County Tyrone Society Pipe Band

County Tyrone Society of New York

Bishop Molloy High School Pipe and Drums

Clan na Gael, Edward Daly Club

Clan na Gael, Napper Tandy Club

Maritime College Band, S.U.N.Y. Maritime College, Fort Schuyler, Bronx, NY

Maritime Emerald Society, S.U.N.Y. Maritime College, Fort Schuyler, Bronx, NY

Edward P. Maloney Memorial Pipe Band

88th Brigade New York Guard

Oakgrove High School Band, Alabama

Young Irelands Camogie

Cork Pipers Band

County Cork P & B Association

Salesian High School Band, New Rochelle, NY

County Sligo S & B Association

County Armagh Pipe Band

County Armagh Association of New York

Pomperaug High School Band, CT

County Tipperary N & B Association

Monaghan Pipe Band

County Monaghan Society

St. John the Baptist High School Band, Babylon, NY

County Clare P S & B Association of New York

Irish Brigade Field Music

Irish Brigade Honor Guard

Peconic Warpipe Band, NY

County Waterford Society of New York

Harrison High School Band, Harrison, NY

County Cavan P & B Association of New York

Friendly Sons of the Shillelagh Pipe Band, NJ

County Donegal Association of NY

Montclair High School Band, NJ

County Longford Association of New York

Clann Eireann War Pipe Band

County Limerick P & B Association

Jamestown High School Band, Jamestown, NY

County Down Association

Curtis High School Band Staten Island, NY

County Wexford P S & B Association

Double R Twirletts, PA

Tri-State All Star Drum & Bugle Corps, Tarrytown, NY

County Galway Association

Northport Pipe and Drum Band

County Derry Society of New York

Lincoln High School Band, WV

County Mayo Society of New York

Knock Shrine, County Mayo Ireland

Middletown North & South High School Band, NJ

County Louth Society of New York

St. Kevin's Sea Cadets Band, NY

Longwood High School Band, NY

County Antrim Society of New York

Ringgold High School, PA

County Kilkenny

West Morris Central High School Band

County Fermanagh P & B Association

Heritage High School Band, Littleton, CO

County Roscommon Society

Main-E-Acts Baton Twirling Team

North Babylon High School Band, Long Island, NY

County Westmeath Association of New York

Rhode Island P. F. Pipe & Drum, RI

County Carlow Association of New York

Maine Twirlers, Maine

Robert Moses High School Band, NY

County Meath Association of New York

Cohoes High School Band, NY

County Kildare Association of New York

The Guard Pipe Band, Warren, NY

Irish Business Organization

Niall O'Leary School of Irish Dancing

Vernon High School Band, NJ

Grand Council of United Emerald Societies

NY Telephone & Communications Emerald

New Utrecht High School Band

NYC Board of Education Emerald Society

Westchester Bus Lines Emerald Society

Thomas O'Shaughnessy Memorial Pipe Band

Suffolk County Firefighters Emerald Society

Spirit of Black Rock Fife and Drum Band

Irish American Building Society

Lebanon High School Band, VA

Saint Edwards University Alumni, TX

Mahopac High School Band, Mahopac, NY

Belmont Abbey College Alumni Association of NY

Marymount University Alumni, VA

Innis Fada Pipe Band

Irish American Society of Nassau, Suffolk & Queens

Northern Westchester & Putnam Counties Pipe & Drum Band

Irish American Social Club of Northern Westchester & Putnam

Nutmeg Volunteers Fife and Drum Corps

Irish Heritage Festival Committee Orange County

Hofstra University Irish Society

Pentucket Regional High School Band, MA

Glasgow Celtic Supporters Club, NY

Out of Town Firefighters

F.B.I. Emerald Society Pipes and Drums

F.B.I. Emerald Society

Francis P. Beirne Division 9 AOH New York County

Formation Committee and Line of March Committee

Photography Credits

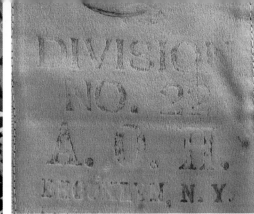
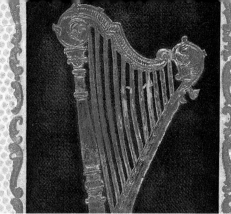